LUCAS Out LOUD

"*Lucas Out Loud* is brilliant stuff. Hilarious, heart-warming and challenging. By the time I'd finished, I felt more glad than ever to be a follower of Jesus."
Andy Hawthorne, The Message Trust

"I know of no other writer who is able to prick the balloon of pomposity that afflicts some parts of the Christian Church – and do it with such humour, gentleness and style – as Jeff Lucas. Jeff is someone who writes truthfully, assuredly, and helps us come face to face with the thing we often try to avoid – reality. *Lucas Out Loud* is a relaxing, refreshing and fascinating read. I loved it and so, I think, will you."
Selwyn Hughes, Life President, CWR

"Rich in wisdom and light."
Adrian Plass

"A gritty, funny, provocative take on how to live Christianly in a complex world – watch out for the seagull!"
Pete Broadbent, Bishop of Willesden

"Compelling, perceptive, irreverent, provocative, frank, vulnerable, comic and disturbingly honest – *Lucas Out Loud* is a tonic to the soul."
Steve Chalke MBE, Founder Oasis Global & Faithworks

"Over the top . . . outrageous . . . uniquely brilliant . . . out on a limb . . . a communicator's communicator. Jeff Lucas has an infectious passion for being culturally relevant. I believe God laughed out loud while Jeff wrote this, and you will too when you read it."
Clive Calver

"In this book 'Laughter' and 'Lucas' become almost synonymous words. But this is far more than entertainment. A brave reality sweeps over the religiosity of many who thought they had found spiritual reality but are being sucked back into play acting again. Like a Shakespearean fool, Jeff Lucas uses self-effacing hilarity to expose the foolishness of us all . . . and then takes us back to God, the rock of realism."
Charles Price

LUCAS Out LOUD

JEFF LUCAS

Copyright © 2005 Jeff Lucas

Reprinted 2006.

12 11 10 09 08 07 06   8 7 6 5 4 3 2

First published 2005 by Spring Harvest Publishing Division
and Authentic Media
9 Holdom Avenue, Bletchley, Milton Keynes, Bucks, MK1 1QR, UK
Box 1047, Waynesboro, GA 30830-2047, USA
www.authenticmedia.co.uk
Authentic Media is a division of Send the Light Ltd.,
a company limited by guarantee (registered charity no. 270162)

British Library Cataloguing in Publication Data
A catalogue record for this book is available from the British Library

ISBN 1-85078-630-5

Cover design by fourninezero design.
Typeset by Temple Design
Print Management by Adare Carwin
Printed and Bound by J.H. Haynes & Co. Ltd., Sparkford

Dedicated to David Bell

You continued to live life out loud
when sickness could have silenced you.

CONTENTS

Foreword ix

A very brief introduction xi

In the details 1

Hugging for beginners 4

Something for the weekend 7

All in the mind 12

Dispatches from the Sahara 21

Lessons from the bathroom 26

Airborne animal farm 30

A little help from my friends 33

Consumer church 37

In search of perfection 40

The spirit of Victor 43

Bad theology 46

Jesus knows about great sex 49

The myth of the superhuman 52

Blaming God 55

Ashes into gold 58

Lying in love 64

Humans like to herd 67

The perils of machines 70

R.S.V.P. 74

The gatekeeper 77

Arthur 80

Careless whispers 84

Father of the bride 87

A confused foreigner 90

False assumptions 95

First impressions 98

David's story 101

FOREWORD

In 1995 I invited a friend to a Christian weekend, hoping that somehow God would reach into his life and bring him to faith. I was also hoping God would do the same for me. Having just completed seven years of theological training, I was washed up and worn out. There I was sitting at the back of a large tent in an August gale and feeling far away from God. I had endured the worship with gritted teeth and prayed that no one would want to hug me or greet me with a holy kiss.

There then came a man to the stage who, at first, I thought had somehow got there by mistake. His words warmed my heart, the tears of laughter rolled down my face, my stomach creased in pain and, in amongst the laughter and the tears, God spoke to me. My friend was also converted. Two people sorted in one day, lives restored, joy felt. The lunatic on the stage turned out to be a man named Jeff Lucas. A John the Baptist, voice for Jesus who isn't afraid to tell it as it is and hold up all of our Christian jargon and frailty to the light of God's grace.

In the pages of this book, Lucas has done it again. This book should come with a health warning. It will change your life, the way you look at God and how we act as Christians. It is packed with deep insights that come from our Father, communicated in a style that chatters pleasantly in your ear – as if you are listening to an old and trusted friend. The pages turn easily. Laughter opens the heart so the Holy Spirit can be heard. I felt warmed and yet challenged, stilled and yet pushed to action.

Above all, Jeff Lucas's honest insights give me the hope that I can be who I want to be in the Lord. Many books have left me with a feeling of condemnation – that somehow my walk with the Lord wasn't good enough and that I could be doing more and more. Looking at the super smiles and bright white teeth emblazoned on the covers of those books made me feel that they were prospering and I was sinking.

Lucas is different. What he writes is real, understandable and uplifting. He does challenge and confront us with our own issues, but always in a constructive way – not to tear us down. He blesses us into action rather than condemning us into a moribund coma.

In his busy and transatlantic-hopping life, Jeff Lucas maintains the strength of faith to hold it all together and hear that still small voice of the Lord – which he puts into words that leap from page to heart. If you are going to read any Christian book other than the Bible, then read this one. It is truly inspired; written in love, honesty and truth; packed with wisdom and coated in joy. This book is a blessing for the family of God, written by one who knows the heart of the Saviour.

G. P. Taylor
International best-selling author of *Shadowmancer,*
Wormwood and *Tersias the Oracle* (forthcoming)

A VERY BRIEF INTRODUCTION

It had been a heartwarming evening: around two hundred hardy souls had showed up on a snowy Tuesday for an evening of storytelling, fun, laughter, challenge and music. (The latter was not provided by me. That wouldn't be good, as my singing prompts people to cry out to God. In anguish.)

I recognized some of the faces in the crowd from countless Spring Harvest Christian conferences; I've spent about a year of my life in conference residences, and some of the regular harvesters are like old friends. Their names escape me, but their smiles are familiar. During the half-time break, I had popped out to the bathroom. My ablutions were interrupted by two somewhat desperate women pounding on the door. Apparently the line for the ladies' room was too long and they had decided to head for the gents. We laughed as I emerged and ended up having a chat and a prayer in the foyer: a God moment, or so it seemed.

But things were about to go downhill fast. I slipped into the back of the church auditorium and sat listening to the musician. Suddenly a man seated in front of me stood up and grabbed his coat. "This is rubbish, and I'm not listening to it any more," he barked and stomped out of the hall towards the foyer. I followed him, genuinely concerned and eager to find out what was wrong. Sometimes people explode with hostility because they are wrestling with enormous issues that sit just beneath the surface of their skins, and it only takes something relatively small to ignite an irrationally hostile reaction. Was he battling huge pain? There are times when being forced to

"This is rubbish, and I'm not listening to it any more"

listen to what might seem like irrelevant preaching can be an experience somewhat akin to Chinese water torture. Perhaps I had made a misguided aside, an unintentionally insensitive comment that had bruised this man. All of this rushed through my mind as I pursued him. But I would never discover the answers to these questions.

As I approached him, he turned both barrels onto me, his face twisted into a sneer. At first he rebuked me for not doing National Service – which I could hardly apologize for, seeing as I wasn't consulted on the date of my birth. Then he targeted my calling and went for the jugular.

"Call yourself a preacher? You're nothing, you're no preacher." He listed some worthy ministers that I should listen to for a few tips. Most of them were dead, except for Billy Graham. His voice got louder and his insults were finely crafted: perhaps he aspired to be an orator. "You use a million words to walk a hundred yards!" he fumed. My heart sank. I felt that I was exactly how he described me – a nothing, just a bumbling, superficial clown. I tried to defend myself – usually a mistake with these types – and his anger turned to threat. "Don't even try, or I'll get *really* angry." This man wanted nothing less than to totally and permanently silence me. Fearing that a heart attack – for him – was on the way, and that the congregation was about to be treated to the unseemly sight of the guest speaker being punched around by one of the church members, I decided to make just one request.

"Before you walk out of this building now, please take my hand and part with me with some grace," I said. He looked hesitant. I insisted. "Please."

I'm not sure it was the right thing to do. Was this unsanctified mercy? He certainly doesn't have to appreciate my musical colleague, or like my approach to communication, but his acerbic rudeness was inexcusable and profoundly un-Christian. Perhaps I should have quietly told him so. But he took my hand, lingered for the briefest of moments, and the hint of a thaw, the glimmer of a smile, passed over his face like a fleeting ghost. But it was gone in an instant. He turned, flung open the door and marched out into the arctic night.

The sudden blast of frosty air filled my chest, and at once I felt overwhelmed by a wave

This was not the first time that my communication style got me into hot water

of weariness. I looked at my hands, which were trembling, and wondered about just quietly leaving to go home, never to darken another pulpit. This was not the first time that my communication style got me into hot water (and it wouldn't be the last). I'm unashamedly committed to telling the truth about my struggles. My mistakes, doubts and fears are fairly well known – anyone looking for an airbrushed hero of the faith would certainly pass me by.

But I want to keep living life out loud: asking awkward questions, confessing embarrassing weaknesses and generally encouraging other people who don't feel they've yet graduated from the human race to keep going for God. And I'm so grateful to have met so many fellow travelers who are committed to living life at volume. I love to laugh – mainly at myself – and to see others smile too.

So not everyone likes it – and they don't have to. But the fact that you hold this book in your hands suggests that you might think that a chuckle or two before death is not only okay, but also what we were made for. What's between these book covers might prompt a few tears too. So I'm not going to shut up, but rather keep doing what I believe God has asked me to do. If you get around to reading this book,

I'll pray that something in it will help you live life out loud too. As I turn the volume up in the next few pages, I'm really asking that you'll hear less of me and more of the voice of Jesus, who I know loves you and me both – and my angry critic too.

With love to you,

Jeff Lucas
Colorado 2005

IN THE DETAILS

Tambourines and testimonies were all the rage when I was a bright young Christian thing. The tambourines were particularly challenging – I would inevitably find myself standing next to an enthusiast with no rhythm. The Bible says something about God's desire that we praise him "on the tambourine," but I've always assumed that he was just being especially kind, giving us the impression that he actually enjoys this.

But I do miss the testimonies. Our Sunday evenings were invariably peppered with lovely moments when we breathlessly passed on the news that (a) God was real and (b) he had showed up yet again on the domestic landscape of our little lives. Admittedly, sometimes the spontaneous nature of the testifying was downright dangerous. Radio stations usually run their "live" shows with a ten-second delay so that they can edit out any unfortunate expletives.

> One evening, a very sincere lady gave thanks for the untwisting of her son's testicles

We, sadly, did not possess that technology, so God was occasionally more maligned than praised by our efforts to tell of what we thought were his deeds. One evening, a very sincere lady gave thanks for the untwisting of her son's testicles, which had apparently, hitherto, been quite knotted. She explained the excruciating untangling at length. A few exuberant souls responded to her good news with cries of "praise the Lord," and some of the men in the congregation just cried. I chose to maintain a fixed grin throughout. And then there were those confusing moments when someone testified that the Lord "had been so good" because, while the rest of her workmates had been smitten with some mysterious plague, "I, hallelujah, have been spared!" While joining in with the rejoicing, I remember wondering if the Lord who "had been so good" in quarantining the testifier had been not quite so good – almost naughty, perhaps – in visiting her colleagues with boils. But, in it all, there was a delightful affirmation that God was interested and indeed entwined in the details of our days. I'm convinced that church should be more about the telling of our little, epic stories. All of which leads me to share my own little "unusual" testimony here.

Most Sunday mornings are busy for me – we have three morning services, so a total of around four and a half thousand people show up expecting a sermon. As a preacher, I live in fear that I will sleep in, oblivious to the demonized shrieking of my alarm clock: an empty pulpit yawns while thousands wait. If this happened, I would be forced to do the gentlemanly thing and throw myself on a nearby sword.

Last Saturday night, I went to bed early and set my alarm as usual. I was exhausted, and constant jetlag was creating havoc with my sleep patterns, which were suitable for a time zone somewhere in the middle of the Atlantic Ocean. In a fitful sleep, I dreamed a very vivid dream – my alarm clock battery died, and I slept through it. I woke up in a cold sweat and glanced across at the clock – which, just as I had dreamed, had stopped some hours before. It turned out to be only five a.m., so, muttering a prayer of thanks for the dream, I replaced the clock battery and set the alarms on two mobile phones too – I was taking no chances.

The question is: did God send a dream to let me know that my clock was useless? I believe he probably did. The idea seems ridiculous, as if heaven is playing games with us. Why should God care about the trivial concerns of well-fed us when most of the world is lean with hunger? God's movements remain mysterious.

Such a gift reminds me that the God who seems to take an interest in our hair count – the same one who notices when even another

The question is: did God send a dream to let me know that my clock was useless?

sparrow bites the dust – is big enough to edge his way into our small stuff, for which I will be eternally grateful. His involvement – not bruising, rough intrusion, but the gentle touch of caring interest – makes me want to praise him.

It's been said that the devil is in the detail. I'm not sure if that's true, but it's good to know that God is.

HUGGING FOR BEGINNERS

I am pleased to propose an idea that will revolutionize the exchange of warm, affectionate greetings at weekly Christian gatherings. Heed these words and incidents of minor injuries will markedly decrease. Crimson-faced embarrassment will henceforth not be so much in evidence on Sunday mornings. The breakthrough suggestion is as simple as this: if you're a member of one of those churches that are into hugging, then, from today, always hug people to the *left*.

Failure to observe this simple guideline has led me into more than my fair share of mishaps. Hugging is always an awkward business – particularly if one is greeting a member of the opposite sex and both holy huggers are committed to maintaining zero pelvic contact. They usually engineer this by both sticking their backsides out. They thereby achieve the very purest of hugs, but their angular embrace looks like a bizarre mating ritual. Hugging challenges don't end there, however: multidirectional hugging has too often led to a bruising head-butt or, worse still, a painful collision of noses. It's hard to feel kindly when one only wants to pick up a hymn book and handshake from that smiling usher but ends up with mild concussion from yet another clash of heads. While these scenes are reminiscent of feuding deer locking antlers, it is essential to not stop grinning.

The potential for red faces increases when a kiss on the cheek is involved as well as a hug. If the other person is going for a peck and you've only signed up for a hug, you end up getting your neck kissed – which is so *excruciatingly* embarrassing for the smoocher, and even more so for the one so kissed. This has happened to me so many times, I've emerged from some extremely cuddly services with more love-bites than Dracula's concubine. All is not always lost: a few minor strains and sports injuries have been sorted by all the shoulder patting (three is usual) and back rubs that usually accompany these hugs – although the application of Deep Heat might sometimes be useful, if not a little smelly.

Of course, we know that all this hugging in church has gone wrong when the younger, and frankly more drop-dead gorgeous, sisters are subjected to protracted seasons of hugging from long lines of grinning brothers who have such an enthusiasm to share "God's love." Leering huggers usually repent quickly when greeted with a Bible verse about lust and a swift, well-aimed kick.

And one should always remember that there is a time and a place for all this embracing. I once knew a giant-sized Anglican vicar who was prone to swan around the city streets in his flowing black clerical robes. His philosophy was, "if it moves, hug it, and do so with great intensity and duration." I developed the habit of crossing to the other side of the road when I saw his smiling head bobbing towards me in a sea of very untactile Saturday morning shoppers. I had been swept into the tent-like folds of his robe one time too many, and held there for way too long while he whispered sincere and genuine Christian greetings into my ear. Passing shoppers were bewildered: why was I passionately embracing the vicar? Some even thought we were evangelists doing some drama and gathered around to see how the scene would end, only to realize that there was no drama at all – just two happy Christians saying hello.

But for all of this embarrassment and confusion, I remain grateful to be part of the warm embrace that is church. If you are in one of those more formal churches where people can barely bring themselves to shake hands and perhaps resort to waving at each other across the pews (not likely to cause injury or create temptation, but perhaps emotionally unfulfilling), then perhaps you might dare to offer a hug here and there. Perhaps you genuinely prefer that no one invades your personal space – and of course you are totally entitled to having that wish respected too.

> **I remain grateful to be part of the warm embrace that is church**

But then some of us perhaps need to inch a little out of our terror of touching or being touched. And we must realize that, for some, Sunday morning may well be their best hope all week for some kind of meaningful contact with other human beings. Churches can be lonely black holes. The sense of isolation that some people feel may be made even more acute by all the talk of love and relationships – while they struggle still with aching aloneness.

Recently I was drawn into a wonderful, extended hug-fest – when speaking at a local church's annual residential retreat.

SOMETHING FOR
THE WEEKEND

Speaking at church weekends used to be a hazardous exercise only to be undertaken by the bravest Christian leader. Christian conference centers were often managed by a Basil Fawlty type with a fish badge on his lapel. The philosophy in the bad old days seemed to be that we Christians were going to enjoy an eternity of bliss in heaven, so we could jolly well put up with a few days of agony in the Gehenna Conference Center in the meantime. We munched on barely edible food, featuring beef obtained from cows that had died in hit-and-run car accidents, and we spooned up semolina puddings more suitable for use as wallpaper paste. These culinary delights were served by stern-faced waitresses who obviously wished they had been issued with a cattle prod. Sometimes the heating broke down, prompting us to consider rubbing a couple of house groups together to keep warm.

We spooned up semolina puddings more suitable for use as wallpaper paste

Complaining about anything back then was useless, since the bearded sister from Latvia who was in charge couldn't understand what we were saying. Mealtimes offered a further challenge: a bell would ring, or a gong would be struck, and a lengthy prayer of grace would follow (often performed by the Latvian lady in her native tongue, so we had no idea whether she was pronouncing blessing, praying for protection for those who would eat the semolina, or muttering a curse in the name of strange gods). Even nibbling at one's food before the mandatory grace was akin to a capital offense and would provoke a wrinkled nose and a grimace of the sort usually reserved for those who make bad smells in public. Not a great way to spend a weekend.

Before I invite a barrage of complaints from the many lovely and dedicated conference center staff around the world (and risk finding myself waking up with a dead horse's head on my pillow next time I speak at one), let me quickly say that things have, for the most part, improved enormously. Hot water is now usually, well, hot. The food is much better and standards are probably at their highest. And what goes on at these weekends is often a whole lot more balanced and sane as well.

> The whole event was like one long, group hug

But this recent church weekend was simply the best. The whole event was like one long, group hug – and they even drew me, an outsider to the church and the guest speaker, into the embrace. Occasionally organizers of such weekends expect their invited speaker to preach ninety-four times, pray and prophesy over every person present and counsel lines of deeply challenged folks during mealtimes. I emerge from events like this exhausted and feeling that atheism is a serious temptation.

This church had developed a great program, though. I spoke only three times. There were other studies and activities going on, but these people were seriously delighted to be together – and not just to sit in rows imbibing yet more biblical information. The Saturday night cabaret was bliss. A child played the violin, and her three notes, delivered with intense concentration, received a rapturous response that Yehudi Menuhin could not have hoped for. Three girls did some tap dancing and collapsed halfway through in a delightful fit of giggles. The loud laughter that greeted unfunny puns, and even the joke of one young lad about an Irishman with flatulence who blew up a building, was an act of love. To crown it all, a lovely older gentleman, who had only come to faith recently, read a poem about how he missed his deceased wife, the one great love of his life. His eyes moist with tears, he broke out into a broad smile after delivering one of what he considered to be his best poetic lines. Pausing for effect, he asked the audience: "That was really good, wasn't it?" They clapped and cheered: it was very good indeed. He sat down, his eyes bright now. For a little while, he was no longer a sad man with a lifetime of fading memories in his head and a worn-out photograph of his darling in his wallet.

For a little while, he was no longer a sad man with a lifetime of fading memories

He had been able to celebrate the one he missed, every minute of every day, with people who cared enough to listen.

During the final session, a lady took the microphone and boldly announced that she had been, in her words, "a consistent pain to the leaders" in what she described as her unkind and hypercritical attitudes. She wholeheartedly apologized to the church family and thanked the leaders whom she felt she had bruised. Tears and yet more hugs ensued.

As I watched them roaring their approval at each other, playing board games late into the night, young and old and everything in between – together – I saw again the beauty of being able to come in from the frigid cold of loneliness, to be at the hearthside of love in the family of God. It's a cold, drafty world, where people often watch *Friends* with unrequited longing; so church at its best is very, very good indeed.

Church can be frustrating, indeed exasperating, at times: but when it is warm, real and affirming, as I saw that weekend, it is really good. Here is a place for the first-year student, who is feeling the loss of being away from home for the first time ever, and who hovers hesitantly on the edge of established friendships. He desperately hopes – and even prays – that someone will invite him home for a pizza or even a cup of lukewarm coffee. Here he can find welcome and warmth.

Here there is a place for the single mother who wakes up every day with the sense that she just doesn't fit. She struggles to invite married couples for dinner, or to go clubbing with the twenty-somethings – but here she connects in a network of relationships.

And here, too, is a place for the divorcee who works late just to avoid the silent house that waits; the word "welcome" is on her doormat – it seems to mock her. She sends herself flowers once in a while: perhaps here there is someone else who will bring her flowers. Perhaps there is someone who will share a meal.

Here we can all be home. So I remain delighted to be part of this glorious, irritating, sometimes thrilling, sometimes dull, family that we call church.

Make sure today isn't a hug-free zone

So, go ahead – with a kindly word, a card of thanks, or an actual embrace – make sure today isn't a hug-free zone for those who bump into you. You will probably make someone's day, or even month. But, please remember: to the left. History may marvel at my contribution to church life; Luther refocused us on justification by faith, and Lucas gave us hugging to the left. Here I stand; I can do no other.

ALL IN THE MIND

I am not the man I used to be. Six months ago I declared war on most carbohydrates and decided that I needed to embrace an exercise regime that involved something more than a stroll to McDonald's and back. I now weigh nearly forty pounds less.

I knew that the time had come for drastic action when just picking up a New Testament was causing breathlessness; lifting a hefty concordance could have wiped me out completely.

Initially things did not go well. As if one diet wasn't enough, I had to go on two diets at first because I didn't get enough to eat on just one. I then embraced that low-carbohydrate regime that requires one to view a slice of bread as if it were something created by Satan to bring planet earth to an end. I have successfully indoctrinated myself. I now find it impossible to walk past the bakery section of my local supermarket without rebuking the loaves therein. Out went cereals (no hardship, as I always felt that the box was more tasty than the contents, if a little more chewy) most fruits (loaded with sugar – how did they get it all in there?) and in came red meat, bacon, eggs and lots of other stuff that I had always feared would slowly but surely kill me. I decided that even if I died of clogged arteries, I'd at least fit into a slim-line coffin. And funereal black makes you look thinner, too. I'd be one trim corpse.

I had to brainwash my taste buds into believing that certain foods taste really good – like low carbohydrate

> I had to brainwash my taste buds into believing that certain foods taste really good

chocolate bars. I'd rather snack on dirt. I mourned the end of a lifelong affair with pancakes and bade ice cream a fond farewell. But I drew the line when the diet demanded that I cut out wine. The Bible orders me to take some for my stomach's sake, and clearly I should obey God's command over the instructions of some diet guru . . .

. . . but the diet began to take effect. I rejoiced in measurable progress when I spotted my feet again. Having shed some flab, it was time to work on the development of some muscle. I even went as far as joining the local gym. I then realized that one was actually expected to attend as well. For a while, my visits were sporadic. My main exercise involved carrying the gym membership card around in my back pocket (if you carry it faithfully for ninety-eight years, you'll burn thirty-five extra calories and have buttocks of steel). The gym was overcrowded with healthy-looking people who apparently poured themselves into their spandex training outfits and looked appallingly good. I wanted to go to the gym only when plenty of puffing and panting fat people were around – or at least folk who were bigger and more breathless than me. This would give me someone to look down on.

If God wanted us to look like the incredible hulk, he'd have given us bigger shirts

I gave up on weight training – the effort required was too great just to end up looking like one of those champion body builders. Such activity can't be natural; if God wanted us to look like the Incredible Hulk, he'd have given us bigger shirts. Beside, all that posing for photos covered from head to foot in grease just didn't appeal. I started power walking. This looks very stupid indeed, with all that purposeful striding and swinging of arms which made me look rather robotic. People would snigger and whisper "Take me to your leader," as I marched woodenly past them. But a little muscle began to appear. All right, it would only be visible under a microscope, but it was a start . . . After becoming a power-walking champion, however, I was ready for a new challenge. Finally, I could stand the humiliation no longer.

Pumped up with "Praise Him in the Perspiration" downloaded on my iPod (okay, I jest) and clad in my red silk all-in-one running suit with a large fish emblazoned on my rear end (I jest again – I wouldn't be seen dead in red), I set about to become a runner. And it was then that I discovered my greatest opponent to date: my own mind.

Running and exercise is difficult, but not because of my knees (strengthened by many thousands of intercessory hours) or my lungs (expanded by much intercessory shouting at principalities and powers, which are either (a) deaf or (b) more likely to get lost when yelled at). It is difficult because I am cerebrally challenged.

Brain power
When it comes to exercise, diet, prayer, Bible reading – or anything else that requires me to make a series of consistent choices, my problem is in my head. When I run, my brain exercises its considerable strength to resist. My mind gets an edge in the battle long before physical weariness begins to assault my body. And how my mind minds me running! Even as I write this, I am dressed in my rather fetching jogging gear – all I need to do is pop on my designer trainers, open the door and run my four-mile daily route. But it's freezing out there. This couch is so very comfortable, it was surely designed just for me while I was still in my mother's womb. There may be grizzly bears, giant

anacondas, or aliens from outer space out there waiting to abduct a runner and take him away on the mother ship. And another cup of tea would be lovely.

And then, if and when I do make it outside, the war begins in earnest. My two operative brain cells send me urgent messages, usually just a few yards into the run, screaming that this whole exercise thing is complete madness, that a man of my age should be reclining on a beach somewhere inhaling a jumbo-sized double pepperoni pizza, and that the best thing to do would be to stop running, *right now*, hail a taxi and head for the nearest Dunkin' Donuts. My mind is capable of many dirty tricks, sometimes resorting to downright intimidation. During yesterday morning's jog, I became convinced of the imminent likelihood of a heart attack, stroke and/or brain tumor if I persisted with my commitment to forward mobility. It was at that point, too, that malaria and an assortment of exotic tropical diseases began to loom. The mind baffles.

A man of my age should be reclining on a beach somewhere inhaling a jumbo-sized double pepperoni pizza

Seasoned runners are well practiced in this mental tug-of-war, and they prepare themselves to hit what marathon competitors call "the wall." You know you've hit the wall when you have nothing left, mentally or physically. You are running on empty, and the road ahead seems utterly desolate. I'm told that you usually run into the wall at around the fifteen-mile mark; I usually slam into a ton of bricks after a hundred and fifty yards. All of my initial mental enthusiasm, which gets me out there in the first place, suddenly drains away – and I am consumed with fervent prayer for the provision of an iron lung. But I don't really need it. My problem isn't to do with stamina, but with that defeated voice that often whispers inside me, urging me to throw in the towel. As one advertisement for athletic shoes puts it, running is me against me. The question is, which part of me will win – the faith-filled, passionate, disciplined me, or the bloke who prefers power lifting with hot dogs?

I hit the proverbial wall in many other areas of my life, too. That same internal nagger insists that I can't pray effectively, and that I am a failure as a husband, parent, leader and friend, and that massive disaster and failure is probably just around the corner anyway . . . so what's the point of trying?

But it is worth trying, so, in addition to fighting flab, building muscle and increasing my stamina, I need to exercise my mind, too. Scripture calls us to think on "whatever is good, pure, honest and of good report." I never really understood what that meant – it seemed that God wanted me to permanently think happy thoughts (and sport that faraway grin often worn by very committed Christians who perhaps should be committed).

Arrest that thought

I'm not into "think positive" slogans – but God calls me to take my thoughts captive, and to place rogue ideas under arrest, rather than just allowing any passing notion to wander into my heart and thereafter engage in a hostile mental takeover. I sometimes forget that my mind is the servant of my soul – and not the other way around. That

> **God calls me to take my thoughts captive, and to place rogue ideas under arrest**

means that the I that is at the core of my being does not have to passively permit anything that meanders into my mind to stroll around freely and unchallenged. Of course, the problem comes when the thought is just too delicious or tantalizing. Lust's tactic is to paralyze our mental defenses with promises of breathless excitement and the luxury of self-indulgence. At that moment, abandonment looks so attractive: at worst, it all seems naughty, but so very nice.

But it's a con. Lust is a tired, tarnished old tart, a beauty that purses her lips for a forbidden kiss and then instantly turns into a mocking crone. And how our minds are stained by her embrace. When we allow the corridors of our heads to be littered with the fetid remains of violence and pornography, our lives will begin to take on the stench of decay, and we will grind away in defeat. Sin, which promises exhilaration, actually leaves us depressed. The bite of the rotten apple always leaves a bitter aftertaste.

Sin, which promises exhilaration, actually leaves us depressed

And there's more than sex to spoil us. When we allow the acidic toxins of bitterness to swill around inside our heads and spend our days obsessed with getting even, we set ourselves up for sadness. And the mind that is fixated on getting more, accumulating and grabbing in the madness that is materialism, will never permit us to enjoy what we have now. We'll squander today dreaming about tomorrow's "richer" horizon – which never seems to get any closer. The more we have, the more we want. Given half a chance, sin will wall us in. We will be unable to see the path ahead, much less run the good race.

Like the marathon runner who knows the wall is coming and prepares for it, it's time to post a sentry at the doorway of our minds. You and I are not at the mercy of our sinful desires.

Washing our brains

There is a myth that some people in the world are being brainwashed. Here is the news: we all are. What are you using to wash your brain every day? Our brains are bombarded with ideas during every waking second. My brain is like a magnet; every time I hear a conversation, read a magazine – anything at all – ideas rush at my head. Advertisers know this. They hand over millions for a thirty-second television commercial because they know that their nagging insistence that I buy their stuff actually works. Trendy Hollywood movie directors insist that their latest cinematic offering (which includes gratuitous sex and violence) actually affects nobody – it's all just harmless entertainment. But, when nobody's looking, those very same tinsel town architects pocket small fortunes from companies who want their cars, their breakfast cereals, their watches to appear in the film for just a few seconds, so impressionable are we.

That's why it is so absolutely vital that I feed my mind on the pure truth of Scripture. When I come to the Bible, I rinse my brain in undiluted truth. I immerse myself in messages from the can-do God who invites me to play a part in his plan, rather than playing around with destructive trivia. I suddenly see life through the 20/20 lens of *his*

> **That's why it is so absolutely vital that I feed my mind on the pure truth of Scripture**

perspective. Bible reading for me used to be the Protestant equivalent of whipping myself – I didn't really want to do it and found it all rather painful (especially Leviticus), but it seemed like the thing that good Christians do. Whenever I attempted those "through the Bible in a year" reading marathons, I invariably hit the wall about February. January would go well, I usually managed to complete March in November, and then it made sense to postpone April until the new year. I felt that a "Read through the Bible in three hundred years" would be a great resource for me.

If I made it into an exercise for the sake of it, I would have no more motivation to persevere than if I were running just to see when and how hard I'd crash into the wall. But when I come to Scripture to find God, to soak in his truth, I focus on what is authentic. I wash my brain in reality.

Similarly, I find that my relationships can help or hinder my mental and spiritual well-being. We've all met people who inspire and invigorate us, while there are others who, after five minutes, leave us feeling in need of a quick chat with the Samaritans. The company we keep is important. I become a whiner when I hang out with whiners for too long, but I have spent years nurturing a few friendships with people I know will challenge, invigorate, confront and comfort me. And it's not just a one-way street about my well-being – I want to be the kind of friend who encourages, who leaves behind me a sense of hope to persevere in the race ahead.

Meanwhile, back to my daily jog. Sadly, all this sweat is not a guarantee of more youthful looks. Out shopping yesterday, we stumbled across a man with a little sideshow who was guessing people's ages – for a small price. I handed over the money, but it was a complete con. He was way off in his estimate of my vintage. Unfortunately there was no money-back guarantee.

I'm forty-eight, and he put me at fifty-three.

For a moment, I was tempted to reach for the donuts. But then I remembered why I run; all that effort is not to simulate some anti-aging drug and enable me to pretend that the advancing years are suddenly retreating. I run to live healthier, and longer – with a clear mind and a body that won't let me down when the schedule is grueling.

For a moment, I was tempted to reach for the donuts

Come to think of it, that's why I need a healthy mind too: better, longer living, that can steer me through the storms. When circumstantial tremors threaten to shake my faith, when the trusted colleague has an affair, or the child my friend prayed for dies in an accident, when God seems very long distant and nothing seems to make sense, Scripture – that we have washed our brains in, understood and lived out – can literally be a lifesaver.

DISPATCHES FROM
THE SAHARA

Brothers and sisters," the wide-eyed worship leader whispered breathlessly into the microphone, "There are times when we feel like we are in a spiritual desert, and, as the psalmist says, 'our soul pants for God.' Friends, the Lord wants our pants."

Some of the gathered worshippers looked even more extra-terrestrial than usual and dutifully dedicated their undergarments to the Lord. Others, less godly and more in tune with unfortunate innuendo, stuffed Bibles into mouths to avoid outright raucous laughter and guffawed at the idea of Big Doris in the front row offering up her bloomers in praise.

But, despite his little gaff, the worship leader was right – without wishing to sound too much like a deodorant, there are those seasons when we feel arid and extra dry. Lately, it's been like that for me: life has been more about the Sahara than Kew Gardens. And the parched feeling has not been helped by the fact that, in my recent experience,

Prayer is hard when it feels like an endless one-way chat

God has been rather silent. Prayer is hard when it feels like an endless one-way chat. Lately my quiet times have been just that. *Very* quiet. And being part of public worship has felt more like serenading the ceiling than a wondrous encounter with the Almighty. I feel like I have placed a telephone call, but have been on hold for a very long time. In silence.

I've never been one of those Christians with a red-hot line to the Master on his desk. I vacillate between admiration and concern for those folks who do enjoy broadband spirituality. They apparently enjoy cozy chats with the Creator throughout every day; their lives are punctuated with mind-boggling revelations, downloaded with speed and ease. Apparently, God is very much on speaking terms with these people, but I am in turn both intimidated by them and then thankful that I am not like them. Are they really closer to God, or just in need of medication? And yet I don't want to join the ranks of the crowd who insist that God is somehow locked in the pages of a book and therefore *never* speaks to us directly, through prophecy, dreams, visions – or any of the other modes that he so clearly describes in his word. I once shared a conference seminar with a speaker who insisted that the gifts of the Holy Spirit were now not in use, and who referred to them in Scripture in the way that one looks at an old, rusty bicycle – once efficient, now not needed, thank you very much. His main argument focused on misguided and immature use of the gifts, and he had more than a few horror stories to illustrate the point. But Scripture makes it abundantly clear that, just because some bring discredit on the gifts of the Holy Spirit, this should never encourage us to abandon them. They are too important, and vital. There have been more than a few moments when a word from God changed my day – and my life. Perhaps there's a middle ground, somewhere between the hotline and the disconnected line: where we do genuinely hear the whispers of the God who loves to speak to us. But right now it feels as if someone has sliced the cable betwixt heaven and me.

There have been more than a few moments when a word from God changed my day – and my life

So just why does God seem somewhat distant right now? The Bible says that he is not shy, disinterested, bored with chatting, too busy, or on vacation in some far-flung solar system. But my dilemma remains, and I am not greatly helped by the standard answer that God often goes quiet on us to make us look for him more – *deus absconditus*. That argument makes it sound like God is playing little more than hide-and-seek – not at all the behavior one would expect from the very best Father of them all, particularly when I'm in pain, lonely and doing my very best to love him even when, at the best of times, he's invisible anyway. Isn't that hard enough, or does God like to pile on the pain by leading me into a massive maze and then abandoning me?

And then there are those who would tell me that the deafening silence is not because God isn't talking, but rather because I'm not posturing myself sufficiently to listen to him. If God seems far away, they chortle, guess who's moved? If you've haven't got a black eye, I'm tempted to respond, guess who'd like to give you one? These are the very same people who insist that, if I'm sick and I'm not healed, then it definitely must be my fault. Thanks a lot – not only do I have a migraine, but also an automatic moral problem. There *are* times when the rush of wind around my ears, generated by the speed at which I hurtle through life, causes me to miss the whisper of God. And of course the choice to deliberately rebel against God will create the effect of us placing our fingers in our ears. But that's not always it by any means.

Ultimately, I have no idea why it is that the spiritual life is sometimes bleak, more about hanging in there than leaping through a swashbuckling adventure. And that's okay. But I am not alone when I'm in the dark. The Bible tells me that, this side of eternity, I "see through a glass darkly," to quote the old King James version. Life will sometimes provide a bewilderingly fuzzy reception rather than a plasma quality digital picture. I shouldn't allow wilderness times to prompt me to wander into cynicism, or its more cancerous cousin, unbelief. I used to think that faith was about life as a clear day, when everything stood out in solid, recognizable shapes and there was nothing vague or indistinct. I had easy answers for everything, most of which were hollow clichés and syrupy slogans. I even knew when Jesus was coming back, having purchased a chart that laid it all out neatly. Now I spend more time in the fog and have become more agnostic – by that I mean less sure of some things – in my older age.

> **Life will sometimes provide a bewilderingly fuzzy reception rather than a plasma quality digital picture**

And it's a relief to know that sometimes – like now – I'm just tired. As I type, I feel the wet blanket of weariness draped over my shoulders. It's not that God has died (or worse, is petulant), or that Satan is alive and well on planet earth *and* camping in my bathroom: I just need a good night's sleep.

And, coming from the culture of existential excitement of charismatic circles where we "feel" and "sense" so much, I am learning profound lessons from my quieter, more contemplative friends. There are times when I need to affirm my faith in God, whatever the weather or circumstances, regardless of my emotions. Even if the landscape seems bare and uninteresting and he seems to be nowhere on the horizon, I can declare my trust in him. I have become envious of those churches where creeds are affirmed weekly and liturgy provides words of depth and faith when people have no vocabulary of their own. There are times when I would love the community around me to put words into my mouth, lest I be struck dumb by isolated doubt.

Sometimes, faith is just a choice to walk into the wind anyway. And many others have taken that chilly trek. The psalmist with pants also talked about the God who "dumped him miles from anywhere" (Ps. 22:1, The Message) but ends that prayer by worshipping anyway, without any clear answers in between. So, it's time to try again. God, it's Jeff here. Are you there?

LESSONS FROM THE BATHROOM

I glanced at my watch and calculated that I had about four minutes before it would be time to preach. About to address a leadership conference that had drawn a few thousand delegates from around the world, I was feeling quite tense. I would certainly have to give the impression that I knew something about something. There was just enough time for a "comfort break," which is the nice, polite euphemism Americans use to describe a dash to the "restroom." (Although the word "toilet" is apparently somewhat offensive in America, personally I could think of better places to take a rest in.)

So I slipped out to the bathroom, which had been equipped with loudspeakers that relayed the service. This was helpful multi-tasking; one could use the facilities and be spiritually edified all at the same time. Very efficient – no time to waste in *this* church.

Suddenly, the loudspeaker crackled and I heard my name: I was being introduced to the conference as the guest speaker, who was coming to give his address *now.* I was not. I was in the toilet, in more ways than one. I hurriedly washed my hands (a good habit that should be adopted by Christians everywhere) and noticed with some dismay that the bathroom had one of those evil hot-air hand driers. Rats. I know that old-fashioned paper towels are probably responsible for the desolation of countless rain forests, but I do despise those driers – particularly the ones with the infrared eyes that you have to wave at in order to make them work. Why do I have to greet a machine in order to get dry – and then stand there in a worshipful "hands lifted up" position for what seems like an eternity?

With hands warm but still slightly damp, I pushed at the bathroom door – which was stuck fast. I pushed harder, but it refused to budge. I kicked it, which didn't help, bruised my toe, muttered something quite bad and felt immediately guilt-ridden for such muttering prior to preaching. But it wasn't looking like I was going to do much

> ## Like a Bible-toting rugby player, I barged at the door with my shoulder

preaching today anyway, incarcerated as I was in toiletry solitary confinement. Like a Bible-toting rugby player, I barged at the door with my shoulder, but still it refused to yield. This being a charismatic conference, I strongly rebuked the door and commanded it to open with a loud, authoritative voice, *right now!* This door was obviously the kind that only opened with prayer and fasting. It woodenly refused. I was stuck, stranded in there, perhaps forever.

And then, suddenly, I noticed another door – behind me. This door opened freely – and was indeed the very door through which I had entered the bathroom in the first place. I had been trying to break into the (locked) utility closet. I made a mad dash for the pulpit, face flushed crimson with embarrassment and bemused by the thought that these conference delegates were hoping that I might shed some light on what God was doing around the world. How should I know? I couldn't even get out of the bathroom.

All of which serves to remind me – and you – that we Christian leaders are ordinary, stupid, thoughtless fellow travelers in the comical crowd called the human race. Perhaps I am just plain stupid, but most of us could probably be used as conclusive proof that we did indeed

There are some leaders who like to give the impression that they are different from the crowd

evolve from apes. There are some leaders who like to give the impression that they are different from the crowd and have graduated from super sainthood. Their prayers are always answered, their vision for the future is consistently sharp and clear, and they seem impervious to sin and temptation – or so they would have us believe.

When I am depressed by the thought that my whole ministry is based on me being an accomplished idiot, I am encouraged by Christians who tell me that they find my commitment to reality and truth to be quite refreshing. Then I stop in my tracks and wonder. What are they hearing the rest of the time? Why should being real be so very surprising?

Some people elevate leaders to superhuman status. I learned that in yet another bathroom encounter. In the bathroom at another church, a gentleman recognized me as I dried my hands (this time on one of those roller towels where one is required to carry out an extensive search for an unused inch of cloth). "Hello – you're Jeff Lucas aren't you? Nice to see you, Jeff – though I must say, I'm surprised to see *you* in here." What did this dear man think that Christian leaders do about these basic human functions? Pray about them?

Leaders who aspire to project a something-other-than-human image need to lighten up and realize that they are still clothed in flesh. And the rest of us need to recognize that those we look to for leadership and sometimes revere are ordinary folk who get tired, fed up, bored, upset and atheistic once in a while. In our humanity we want to make some people *special*, just because they stand on public platforms or write books – and therefore a few more people on planet earth are familiar with their names. Sometimes this can be difficult to deal with, even in the tiny goldfish bowl that is the Christian world. Occasionally I am unnerved by the power of my smallest, apparently insignificant actions. Without sounding pretentious, I'm aware that a few people in Christian circles know who I am; some think I'm a so-called "famous Christian" and treat me differently when they put the face to the name. This can make me feel pressure – for I know just how very, very ordinary I am. Sometimes I fear that people would be really upset if they knew the real me. God does know me and, thankfully, he still likes me – which keeps me going. He's the only celebrity worth our admiration.

> This can make me feel pressure – for I know just how very, very ordinary I am

A couple of weeks ago, I attended a small dinner party. One of the guests was a delightful Muslim gentleman who carried some rather impressive credentials. Once the Foreign Minister of Pakistan and educated at Eton, Harrow, Oxford and Harvard, he had played for his national cricket team and was a visiting professor at some of the world's most prestigious universities. He has rubbed shoulders with royals and presidents and is an internationally respected author and lawyer. And he shared some wisdom that we all knew, but needed to confirm. "I discovered that, whoever I met, they are all just people, just ordinary people like us."

Amen to that. And never forget it.

AIRBORNE ANIMAL FARM

A seasoned and weary air traveler (nearly a million miles clocked up in recent years) – I have discovered the existence of the frequent flier fish. I jest not. Boarding today's short hop from Denver to Oregon, the crowded tedium was suddenly and delightfully shattered by the news that a passenger had tried to board his pet goldfish. The flight attendants initially protested, insisting that such an act was dangerous in these days of heightened security (after all, that goldfish might jump out of its plastic bag and bite someone). The disgruntled passenger insisted that, under federal regulations, he was entitled to travel with his permanently gawping companion – "for emotional support." The flight crew dutifully consulted the airline manual and announced to all of us (again, this is absolutely true) that passengers *in need of emotional support* may actually board the plane with fish, cats, dogs, pigs, monkeys and *small horses*. My mind raced as the smiling flight attendant quoted the holy rule book. Would the horse have to use a seat belt? What about toilet arrangements? Or would the equine traveler be free to scatter steaming parcels throughout the plane? Would it be offered a choice of chicken, beef or hay? And during longer flights, would small children be allowed to ride up and down the aisles in a high-altitude gymkhana?

Then it occurred to me: someone, somewhere in government, takes the basic need that we all have – of emotional buttressing – very seriously indeed. Of course,

Passengers in need of emotional support may actually board the plane with fish

the practicalities of it all make the regulation somewhat absurd. A pig couldn't watch an in-flight movie. The earphones wouldn't fit.

And I wondered how well we Christians do when it comes to propping each other up when we need it. We are the ones who have heard the biblical injunction to bear each other's burdens – so how well do we do in the being supportive department?

Few of us are emotional flatliners – and be wary of those who say they are, especially if their surname is Lechter. There are some happy clappies who appear to live life as positive,

> A pig couldn't watch an in-flight movie. The earphones wouldn't fit

mildly ecstatic enthusiasts. If their feet were run over by a truck, they'd rejoice at the savings in their slipper budget – but even they go through bumpy, turbulent times when life seems more black and white than Technicolor. In our proximity, right now, there are people who are having a hard time. Do we notice them?

Perhaps we should spare a special thought for those whose life work is being a prop to others. In your church there are probably full-time carers, who lovingly squander their days on bathing, toileting, changing and wiping the fevered brows of those bedridden loved ones who cannot fulfill these basic functions

> Yet they, too, need a shoulder to cry on once in a while

of life unaided. Those quiet saints, heroes even, are often overlooked because they have developed a reputation for being strong and selfless. They have become the victims of their own perceived strength. Yet they, too, need a shoulder to cry on once in a while. It's better to give than receive – but to endlessly give and *never* receive is an exhausting business.

And what about those who pastor and lead us, those that we expect to support us through our trials? Sometimes we don't see past the clerical collar to the person who wears it. It never occurs to us to ask how they are doing. We rather expect them to be just fine, because that's how they are supposed to be. Why don't we stun them once in a while by being interested in their lives, rather than insisting that we be their continuous preoccupation and obsession?

There are a few people in my life who are nothing short of priceless. They are proud of me when I do well, firm but kind with me when I don't, and they are treasures simply because they are genuinely concerned about me.

Providing emotional support isn't rocket science. It often means little more than listening, smiling, empathizing, praying and letting people know that in a cold, anonymous world, they actually matter. It costs nothing at all, except a few seconds of our time – to go out of our way to be grateful, kind, encouraging, and to ask some caring questions about others that demonstrate that we have something more than us on our minds. And some of us need to take what appears to be a huge, risky leap to let someone else know that we're struggling.

Federal regulations aside, I'd hate to think that someone I know or could have cared for had to rely on a *goldfish*.

A LITTLE HELP
FROM MY FRIENDS

This is the day of the expert.

Just about anytime something significant – or insignificant – happens on planet earth, an army of experts and consultants pops up and tells the rest of us nitwits precisely what has happened, why it has happened and what we should all think about it. A major outbreak of foot warts amongst the penguin population of the obscure island of Arktavik would signal the appearance of a clever chap in an anorak. He has spent his entire waking life studying the podiatry challenges of our waddling, waiter-like friends. This is the moment he has been waiting for.

But there are times when experts can be very helpful. I am grateful for the considered comments of experts during an election, a disaster, or an emergency that calls for a thoughtful, measured response. Experts can save lives, steering us away from emotional, knee-jerk reactions that make us feel good when the world is in peril but actually do little to practically help. If I were injured in a car accident, I'd prefer that a paramedic showed up rather than an enthusiastic first aider. A cancer scare would prompt me to dash off to the nearest *specialist* at speed.

> I write this article from the snow-caked slopes of Breckenridge, Colorado, which (impossibly) is even colder than Skegness

And in my domestic life I am occasionally grateful for experts, like today. I write this article from the snow-caked slopes of Breckenridge, Colorado, which (impossibly) is even colder than Skegness, England, although slightly more beautiful. Breckenridge is home to some of the best winter sports in the world – and it attracts some of the worst winter sportspersons in the world, too. Like me.

I am thinking about changing my name to Eddie. My skiing skills are surely reminiscent of Eddie the Eagle, the ill-fated, utterly useless ski jumper who became famous for being not terribly good at skiing. Compared with my skills on the snow, the man is a master. Skiing is supposed to be a graceful, smooth art, as skier and snow bond together in beautiful unison. I came downhill yesterday looking like someone who was being shocked with twenty-thousand volts every three seconds – there was so much jerking and agitation. One spectator looked alarmed when he saw me coming and enquired in a very loud voice if I was having a seizure. I responded that I was not, and that I was simply having fun.

The only positive thing about all this is that I have brought prayer to the slopes. Tearing downhill completely out of control, and getting perilously close to kissing a cable-car pylon at speed, I engaged in loud, unashamed and high-pitched intercession, which I am sure was a fine Christian testimony to every other skier for miles around. The prayer wasn't terribly profound, though.

The only positive thing about all this is that I have brought prayer to the slopes

It went something like: "Ooooohhhhhhhh Godddddddddd heeeeeeeeeeeellllllllpppppp mmeeeeeeeeeeeeeee…….." Time will tell if this tiny evangelistic seed that I have sown so publicly will bear fruit in the shape of converts dressed in thermal clothing. I missed the pylon and decided to seek some expert assistance in the shape of a skiing instructor. He appeared in the shape of a blond, bronzed god whose smile was whiter than the snow and who had muscles in places where I don't even have places.

Thor's assumed name is James, and he knows his stuff. He asked me how advanced I was. I threw my pride off the mountain and informed him that I knew how to put my skis on. He then showed me that I had my boots on too tight. But major progress has ensued. In just two hours he showed me how to turn smoothly, how to posture myself as I go over major bumps (two inches and more . . .) and, most importantly, how to stop without prayer. James is an expert, he has shown me the moves, and now life is better – and probably longer – because of him.

> **It's impossible to live without encountering a few bumps and bruises**

There are times when we could all use a little help. Life, like skiing, is a challenging sport; it's impossible to live without encountering a few bumps and bruises. It's particularly galling when others go zipping past us and make it look easy. Life can feel like trudging up a mountainous slope – which is even more difficult when others seem to be able to ride the lift up to the alps of quick success. Sometimes we slip and slide our way through the icy terrain of relational conflicts, when warm smiles are replaced by frosty glares. And then there are those late afternoon seasons when the fog comes down, you don't have a clue where you are – and you wonder if you're going to go over the edge into the abyss. We could all use a little help.

The question is, are we able to concede that we could use that help? Some people stopped learning years ago, and the thought that someone else might be able to offer a hand appalls them; they are just too clever, too consummately gifted – in their own eyes. They declare large areas of their lives off-limits to the counsel of others – they reject wisdom that could prevent a major tragedy. This inability to be taught can often be seen among Christians – particularly the more hyper-spiritual sorts who are so chummy with Jesus that they don't need anyone else's help, thank you very much.

In the meantime, I'm off to the Siberian chill of the slopes again. My instructor is taking a lunch break so, for a while, I'm on my own. Like Eddie the Eagle, I believe I can fly. Someone call an ambulance.

CONSUMER CHURCH

Very good. One grilled swordfish with ricotta and wild mushrooms; one seared lamb cutlet with raspberry coulis and dill pancakes; one Balinese chicken satay with mint, lemon grass and peanut sauce; one steak, between rare and medium rare, no more than thirty seconds over, yes, I'll tell the chef, sir, with figs and gorgonzola but on the side; one vegetarian couscous with organic goat's cheese and asparagus tart . . ."

The waiter grimaces a false smile through gritted teeth and turns to me. "And now . . . what would *you* like, sir?"

Everyone else around the table has ordered their chosen meal in oh-so-certain tones, and now panic overwhelms me. It's my turn to do some high-speed deciding. Everyone looks at me with pitying eyes and I glance back, desperate for their help. When dining in a large group I turn into a lemming-like follower, struggling through a thick fog of indecision. The waiter rolls his eyes and shifts from one foot to another. He holds a pencil over his order pad, willing me to make up my mind sometime before the apocalypse. Part of my problem is that I want to know what everyone else will be eating before I decide, lest I make a rash choice and then end up dining with regret, or, worse still, stealing food off their plates – during the closed-eyes moments of saying grace, perhaps. I do hope the marriage supper of the Lamb will be a fixed menu without choices. If not, eternity is going to be *very* long.

And going out for breakfast, particularly in America, is always a particular challenge – simply because of the huge range of choices. My head spins. What toast do I require – white, wheat or rye? And my eggs – how do I want them served? Surely on a plate would be good. But no, there are a plethora of confusing options in the fruit of the chicken department: do I want eggs over-easy, sunny-side up, poached, boiled or scrambled? I sometimes break out into a nervous rash just trying to get my order sorted.

Do I want eggs over-easy, sunny-side up, poached, boiled or scrambled?

Consumerism in every area of life is now the order of the day on both sides of the Atlantic: generic is out; multi-choice is expected in everything. Burger King insist on not insisting, offering instead to serve you cooked cow *your way*. But I wonder if we are allowing that attitude to seep into our attitudes to church life. Quietly but firmly placing my preferences on a throne, I demand that "my" church be tailor-made to *my* order; I'll sniff haughtily and opt out of worship if you don't play the music and style of my choice, which of course is surely God's preferred choice too, since *I* like it. I opt in and opt out according to how *my* needs will be met; and the worship leader becomes a human jukebox waiting for my coin.

Perhaps we should divide our church building up like restaurants do in terms of smoking preferences. Ushers could proffer the menu of choices as we enter the building. Would we like to sit in "clapping," this morning, or perhaps a nice spot in "non-clapping" would be more to our taste?

How about a seat in the broadly quieter zone at the back (safely distant from the Muppet who is playing the drums too enthusiastically, no offering basket passed around in that section and Gladys the odd "prophetess" definitely excluded).

You can now actually find churches that do their best to cater to your every whim. You worship in a room according to your worship-style preference, and the sermon is piped in.

Sometimes we dress up our rank consumerism in the disguise of pursuing the radical for the sake of heaven above – when in fact we are really on safari to try and find what suits us right down to the ground. That's why I have become less interested in pursuing change in the church, unless it is mission-driven change that will make us more effective in getting the good news out.

Of course we will always have our preferences

Of course we will always have our preferences – but when we enthrone them, we end up believing that the church exists for us and, worst of all, Jesus himself becomes yet another someone that we seek to manage and manipulate. Church consumerism quietly but firmly insists that Jesus be our subject rather than our sovereign.

The church is a family, not a facility, with him at the head, not us. Irritated by some minor details in your local church? Do yourself, others and God a big favor. Get over it.

IN SEARCH OF PERFECTION

Call me sad if you like, but I used to be a great fan of the television series *The Darling Buds of May*. I'm not sure why: was it the warm, winsome portrayal of balmy English days with sunshine on your back and lashings and lashings of cream on everything, or the even more glorious vision of Catherine Zeta Jones as the quintessential English rose? Perhaps it was the sight of Pop Larkin (David Jason) and his gathered family, ending every day happy and relaxed as he surveyed the scene and declared it to be "perfick": Larkinspeak for perfect. The idea of the *perfick* is rather appealing.

And so I decided that my recent trip to the Caribbean was going to be the most *perfect* time. I had been invited to speak to a church that was located on an exotic, sundrenched island. I prayed about the invitation extensively (2.3 seconds flat) and felt that the Lord was indeed asking me to respond to this difficult task. My wife Kay and I decided that we would combine this trip with some holiday time. This was going to be absolutely wonderful – bliss indeed.

And it was indeed. The people in the church were delightfully warm and welcoming, and the island was, to coin the phrase, absolutely fabulous.

Almost. Not quite.

It all started to go wrong the very first evening. Overwhelmed by the gorgeous sunset, and delighted that our accommodation was actually on the beach, Kay and I decided to do the romantic thing and sit on the waterfront to watch the sun

At dusk, millions of tiny sand fleas, mostly invisible to the naked eye, appear to look for supper

put his hat on for the day. I smiled at her as she perched uncomfortably on a rock; I stretched out on the beautiful white sand, unaware that, at dusk, millions of tiny sand fleas, mostly invisible to the naked eye, appear to look for supper. The fleas lined up, dutifully said grace and then starting munching on my legs. The next morning I had so many bites, and my legs were so swollen, I looked like the elephant man. Kay smiled at me as I dabbed them with ointment. Mmm. Not quite so perfect.

We decided to go on a submarine ride which, since we didn't drown we thought went rather well. But during the course of the ride we learned all about the source of the gorgeous white sand on the impossibly beautiful beaches. A marine biologist advised us that the parrot fish (this is no joke) bumps up against coral (they do it continuously apparently, it's a hobby), ingests the tiny coral particles and then excretes the remains as sand. It seems that forty per cent of the sand on the island is produced by this rather dubious method. It took the romance out of sitting on those exotic beaches, to know that I was in fact perched atop a huge mound of fish poo. Mmm again.

I was in fact perched atop a huge mound of fish poo

All of which proves once again that, this side of eternity, there really is no such thing as perfection. We ponder glorious photos in holiday brochures – but, when we arrive, the place never looks quite the same. The reality, without computer-generated photo enhancement, never looks as picture-perfect as the glossies suggest.

More seriously, there are no perfect children, no perfect marriages – and (for sure) absolutely no perfect churches. Why do some of us spend our lives on perfection safari, staying in a church/friendship/marriage just long enough to bump into the fish excreta, and then moving on, always mildly disgusted, ever disappointed and never quite finding what we're looking for? The church is not a pristine, gleaming trophy case, but a field hospital loaded with people in the renewal process: and bloody and messy it often is, too.

There are no perfect leaders, no perfect church members. We're all a bunch of flawed human beings, most of us doing our best, staggering around and often missing the target more than we hit the bull's-eye.

So lighten up, give others a bigger break and compromise a little. We did, and we discovered that paradise doesn't have to be perfect to be wonderful. If we do that, we'll discover that even sitting on glorious white fish poo can be very nice indeed.

THE SPIRIT OF VICTOR

I think that I am turning into Victor Meldrew.

Victor, for those who haven't met him, is the poker-faced and eternally grumbling misery who staggers from one calamity to another in the now discontinued *One Foot in the Grave*. His capacity for ineptitude is only surpassed by his legendary ability to complain; his catchphrase is "I don't *believe* it." For the ever-clucking, tut-tutting Victor, life is nothing more than a series of continuous irritations, all of which he both expects and yet is seemingly surprised by. He seems convinced that someone, somewhere is plotting to mess up his life – hence my terror at the thought of becoming like him. Victor definitely affects others around him. His wife suffers long because she lives with him. I commented to my wife Kay recently that, as a preacher, I sometimes get fed up with the sound of my own voice. She smiled and said that she understood how I felt.

But there are other obvious parallels. Many Meldrew-esque mannerisms manifested themselves during a seven-day trip to England recently. I love England, with its rolling green hills, real ale pubs, bad-tempered landlords and petrol prices that require one to take out a mortgage before filling the tank, but the ever worsening traffic jams cause me disquiet – actually, they drive me mad.

Road congestion threatens to turn me into an atheist, and a miserable one at that

Road congestion threatens to turn me into an atheist, and a miserable one at that. Twice in two days I sat fuming on the M25 (surely a highway that is an artery of Satan), fingers drumming on the steering wheel as I crawled tortoise-like through yet another set of road works. Having traveled two miles in two hours, I muttered my frustration to absolutely no one in particular – the car being empty save for the omnipresent God and myself. My prayers that the juggernaut in front of me be removed and cast into the depths of the sea went unheard. I was irritated more than I'd like to admit.

Of course, we all have those days, but being irritated can become an addictive habit. Some of us have apparently made a life choice to be frustrated, and even offended, from birth. If we could have, we'd have slapped the midwife who delivered us. Life before birth was so much simpler; all you had to do was bob around in the womb, suck your thumb occasionally, smile for the scan photo and entertain the folks outside by occasionally kicking your mother. Easy peasy. And then one day you take a short, neck-twisting trip, whereupon some medical vandal cuts your food tube off at the naval, tips you upside down and smacks you until you cry. And the irony of it all is that one is then required to celebrate this day of pain with cake and cards every year thereafter: madness, to be sure. Look at life like that and you're a Meldrew, whose dying words will probably be a breathless complaint about hospital food.

So how does one get delivered from the spirit of Victor? Surely one answer is to realize that Christians aren't promised that they will escape the boring bits of life. They get colds, bank statements with red numbers, sore feet and delayed in traffic. It's not all part of the dark plan to bring us down; it's just another day of life.

And surely another help is to compare our tiny skirmishes into irritation with the really vexing, and indeed heartbreaking, challenges that others around the world face. Being held up on a car-jammed road is a small price to pay for living in a situation where most of us have enough food. Phil Collins is right – most of us spend life, in comparative terms, in what is another day in paradise – particularly in a world that has now learned the meaning of the word "tsunami." So, when we are tempted to go into emotional

Being held up on a car-jammed road is a small price to pay for living in a situation where most of us have enough food

meltdown about something trivial, should we actually stop and consider that it's really not such a big deal and pause to pray for those who face real terrors? We could do worse.

Ultimately, griping is a huge waste of life. We can live our whole lives quite literally with one foot in the grave. Is that the way we're supposed to be? I don't believe it.

BAD THEOLOGY

When I decided to become a follower of Jesus, I had to face up to a somewhat intimidating list of possible consequences that would come my way because of that decision. I might lose some friends (I did, although it was mainly as a result of my zealous habit of delivering text-peppered monologues about God without pausing for breath). I knew that my habit of being the first person drunk at every party would have to go (being drunk at all, I mean, not just being the first one legless past the post). I might be ridiculed for my newfound faith (I was), and my priorities would have to change (they did). But there was one element of the Christian life that was presented as a warm promise, but has since

The assumption was that I would have joy at all times

become something of a burden. The assumption was that I would have joy at all times. The hope – and the veiled requirement, therefore – was that I would be as happy as the proverbial lark, 24/7. Coupled with this was the idea that if I didn't have a smile in my heart at all times, then the problem was "spiritual."

This has proved to be a major challenge. That's not to say that I haven't had more than my fair share of laugh-out-loud days. I remain as grateful as ever that I have been delivered from the numbing meaninglessness of life without Jesus at its heart. But I have frequently felt bowed low by dark, troubled seasons when a profound sadness seeped through every part of me – and the massive pressure to be happy as a Christian bowed me lower. Some years ago I went through a couple of years of clinical depression. I would have felt no shame for wearing a cast on a broken arm, or taking tablets to cure gout – but when I took the pills that were prescribed to break my gloom, I felt like I was sipping the poison chalice of betrayal. Me, a Bible-believing Christian leader, depressed. My guilt was illogical, but real enough. During these periods of twilight, Christianity – or, more specifically, my version of it – made me feel worse, not better, and brought bruises rather than healing. My false expectation that faith would give me a daily emotional high, as well as my refusal to seek medical help when I was in the depths, deepened the shadows in my soul. Bad theology is a harsh taskmaster.

But my skirmishes with damaging theology are nothing compared to what Jane has endured. She is eighty years old now and has been married to a minister for sixty of them – but she spent the majority of her life blind. Literally. When she was a young wife and mother, bleeding in her eyes resulted in severe cataracts, which brought total blindness. Darkness descended. But then Jane had a dream in which God told her, she says, that he was going to help and heal her. She interpreted that dream to mean that she should not seek any medical help, even though her family begged her to consult a physician. She was of the pentecostal type that is wary of doctors and preferred that her recovery come more directly from heaven. This was the way that she had been taught, and she was sticking with it. Her grandchildren were born – but she never saw them. When her hair fell out she started wearing an ill-fitting wig – she didn't

Some mornings she would wake wondering why she didn't have enough faith to see

know, she didn't care. She couldn't see a thing. She spent fifty years blind, but that was surely not the full extent of her suffering. Some mornings she would wake wondering why she didn't have enough faith to see. She apologized to God for what she thought was her faithlessness, and then sometimes she blamed him. At times, loving friends urged her to see a doctor and she would toss and turn through sleepless nights, wondering if they were offering her wisdom – or the poisoned chalice of compromise. There were times of joy, punctuated by seasons of deep sadness.

I don't know how she arrived there, but one day she ended up in the clinic of her family doctor.

"We could take care of those cataracts for you, you know," he gently suggested, aware of her religious scruples.

She hesitated.

"I'm a Christian, just like you," he pressed. "Do you believe that I have a valid ministry as I help people with their ailments?"

She reluctantly agreed.

"Then would you consider that God could heal you – and use me as an instrument in your recovery?"

Twenty-four hours later, the bandages were off and she had 20/20 vision. The grandchildren graduated from being voices only and she set eyes on them for the very first time. She told her doctor that he was better looking than she had imagined. And she dumped the atrocious wig.

Twenty-four hours later, the bandages were off and she had 20/20 vision

But, more importantly, she got rid of the false beliefs that had kept her bound in a prison of corrupt ideas for five decades. Be careful about what you believe. If we're going to live by and die for anything, let's make sure that it's God's honest truth. Other ideas might promise us light, but keep us in darkness for life.

JESUS KNOWS ABOUT GREAT SEX

Today I went where this man had not gone before – to the Sexual Health Clinic at my local hospital. To still your speculations, let me just say that I was there for routine blood tests for a man of my age. Alas, the days of the Genito-Urinary department are ended; this is the era of the starkly named *Sexual Health Clinic*.

All of which makes the place a fearsome place to be. The fact that one is parked there gives the hint that one might be sexually *unhealthy*, and so I sat for two excruciating hours in the men's waiting room, eyeing up the other patients, us all knowing what each other was thinking. What has he got? How did he get it? Is it catching? There was stony silence in that place, and no one actually caught anyone's eye. I suppose that this is not the venue for casual conversation: 'So then, what kind of rash do you have?'

I suppose that this is not the venue for casual conversation . . .

Instead, we stared at the incongruously placed and much thumbed Good Housekeeping magazines with zealous focus. And then I wondered what monsters of fear stalked behind the wooden expressions. The man who was reading the leaflet about HIV hidden behind his *Motors with Hooters* magazine; was this a matter of vague interest, something to read while he waited – or something more?

Some people dealt with the ordeal by being brazen, like one young lady, fresh from her consultation, who rushed into the reception area. She told her boyfriend the excruciating details of her gynecological examination, in a loud, laughing voice that all could hear. We winced, looked away, and crossed our legs. He hushed her to be quiet, and turned crimson red.

But the most telling moment was when a couple more ladies showed up and were searching for the ladies' waiting room. It was thoughtful of the hospital's architects to design separate male and female waiting areas; it was so very brain dead of them to organize the layout of the building so that ladies can only get to their reserved room after passing through the men's area. One of the pair, embarrassed beyond belief that she was even in this place, covered her head and literally ran through the men's lounge. She had to endure architecture that shamed. The medical staff did a marvellous job at trying to put people at ease, but still, for some who were perhaps reaping an unwelcome harvest from the wild oats that they had sown, the pain was more than physical.

> If you're a normal Christian, there will be times when you wonder if all this talk and teaching on morality is very relevant

In a moment, I saw the truth about our so-called free, promiscuous culture. We live in a time when Carrie Bradshaw from *Sex in the City* 'knows good sex'; but does she? Her friend in the series, Miranda, is confused when asked about how many sexual partners she's had. When asks for a number, she pauses, runs out of fingers counting and says, 'You mean this year?'

Their jaunty New Yorker singles lifestyle is painted in rich colours; it looks tantalising, and, if you're a normal Christian, there will be times when you wonder if all this talk and teaching on morality is very relevant. On some lonelier nights, you might secretly crave a life where hormones could take the lead rather than concerns about holiness, and abandonment looks way more attractive than self-control. But the free and easy lifestyle is neither free nor easy. It's important to say this, as sin tarts herself up to be quite the looker and our heads are so easily turned. Just recently, I viewed an American television commercial that showed a blissful looking couple horse-riding on a sunset kissed beach. As the orchestra soared, I wondered what product was being hawked. A slogan appeared on the screen: 'Having choices.

Jesus, not Carrie Bradshaw, knows a recipe for great sex

That's freedom.' The product was a drug that relieves the symptoms of genital herpes; incurable, but some help to prevent outbreaks is available. Not really quite so wonderful; perhaps some of the more honest folks waiting in the Sexual Health Clinic would agree.

Jesus, not Carrie Bradshaw, knows a recipe for great sex. It involves faithfulness, vintage love and the insistence that you will only give your body to the one to whom you've already given your heart. There's forgiveness for the fallen, and grace for those who'd quite like to. Above all, let's know that there are many good reasons for following Jesus, but one of them is simple.

He's got it right.

THE MYTH OF THE SUPERHUMAN

Wisdom is not usually found printed on the front of T-shirts. I recently spotted one designed especially for children, which introduces the wearer as a 'FUTURE PRESIDENT OF THE UNITED STATES.' Considering the limited vacancies for that particular role, one can only imagine how many budding world leaders will be disappointed when they're denied access to the Oval Office.

Another offering, of the more Christian variety, yells 'DON'T GET CAUGHT DEAD WITHOUT JESUS!' which is a subtle nudge towards considering God while one is still in possession of a pulse. Of course those who don't share our faith like to answer back, as evidenced by the somewhat cheeky pagan T-shirt: 'IF YOU CHRISTIANS ARE OFF TO BE WITH JESUS, CAN I HAVE YOUR STUFF?'

But my pet T-shirt peeve award has to go to the 'IF YOU CAN DREAM IT, YOU CAN DO IT' shirt that I saw recently. Ironically, the wearer was swathed in an extra-extra large size so, without being unkind, apparently they aren't dreaming about giving up pork pies any time soon. But, more seriously, I am disturbed at the notion of the mighty human who is limited only by the capacity of their imagination, the saviour called self who can fix just about anything with a snap of the fingers. The 'If I can think it, I can do it' philosophy is patently untrue. I dream of having a deep,

> I am disturbed at the notion of the mighty human who is limited only by the capacity of their imagination

tonally perfect singing voice. Reality means that any future album release from me would probably be called *Songs the Lord rejected*, and sales would be limited to one – my mother, and she'd soon be asking for her money back. Pavarotti I am not, and never will be.

Another little fantasy of mine would be to appear in a film and speak those immortal lines, 'Bond. James Bond.' Alas, even if Pierce Brosnan, Roger Moore, Sean Connery and even the ill-fated George Lazenby were all killed at an ex-007 reunion, still no Hollywood mogul is going to knock on my door. I can dream as much as I like: it isn't going to happen, seeing as I lack one or two essential qualifications for the role, like hair.

It's a bit of a shock to discover that there is a horizon to our abilities

But it seems almost blasphemous to suggest that humanity has limitations. We have come to expect that the cancer will be cured, that the personal debt problem will be resolved (just call the free phone number), and the need, whatever it is, will be met. It's a bit of a shock to discover that there is a horizon to our abilities. So it was in the disaster of Hurricane Katrina's maelstrom ride through Louisiana and Mississippi back in September. I am writing this shortly after, so the questions about inept leadership and bungled relief efforts that cost lives are still being asked – and rightly so. But I was shocked, not only by the awesomely awful video footage that came out of the flood zone, but also to see that even the richest, strongest country in the world was simply overwhelmed by the monster that was Katrina. Watching endless footage of tearfully distraught survivors stranded in the Superdome, I yelled at the television screen and demanded of no one in particular that helicopters should be sent in, police be dispatched, and food and water instantly appear. I forgot that there are only so many helicopters, some of the police weren't answering their calls and had opted for a career change and that a relief operation of this size will include delays and blunders. Absolutely no excuses for incompetence here; but even when human ingenuity sparkles and the response is meticulously methodical, none the less, we mere mortals sometimes just can't cope. Living on this sin-spoiled out-of-kilter planet is a dangerous matter. Mother Nature is no kindly parent who can be easily tamed by little us. We can't control the weather in the sky, finally banish the weeds in the garden, or swat the little worries that buzz around our brains like pesky mosquitoes. In our falleness, we can't pick ourselves up.

In short, we are in need

In short, we are in need, which is why the messianic medic has come to tend to us all – because at our best, we're casualties.

So if you're a perfectionist, lighten up a little. Ask for help without shame, and know that failure doesn't have to be tragic. Pray for grace to hold on to hopefulness and yet lower your expectations; don't be quite so surprised when humans around you do what comes naturally – being human. Even those we love the most won't always please us. Like my mother, who just phoned.

She bought my album. I owe her 14.99.

BLAMING GOD

The lady stood to "prophesy" with a characteristically trembling voice and a breathless, dramatic air. "Thus says the Lord," she declared (always a mistake, in my book – that's for the hearers to decide, not the "prophet"). "Just as Moses led the animals out of the ark two by two, so I shall lead you, says the Lord . . ."

Mass confusion swept over the congregation, who were now completely befogged. Was God saying that he was going to lead them forth like a bunch of camels and water buffalos, following a lengthy cruise? And, more importantly, was it not Noah who had presided over that ancient march with various domestic pets and wild animals?

Furtive whispers were exchanged in the pews. "It was Noah, wasn't it? I'm sure it was Noah . . ." The more "spiritual" people muttered: "Perhaps she's slightly in the flesh." More carnal people – or perhaps sane people, depending on how you measure these things – were more direct in their appraisal. "She should get medical advice . . . God knows she needs it."

Two hundred sets of buttocks clenched in fearful anticipation as again the familiar mantra was intoned

But wait! More was forthcoming. Five minutes after rewriting the biblical narrative of the flood, the dear lady stood to her feet to prophesy once more. Two hundred sets of buttocks clenched in fearful anticipation as again the familiar mantra was intoned: "Thus says the Lord . . ." The speaker identified herself once more. "*I the Lord* am mistaken . . . it was Noah."

And then she sat down, surely convinced that Almighty God could make a mistake before she could. In this little moment of madness (and I say this as a fully-fledged charismatic with a great love for the gifts of the Spirit), she was guilty of doing what is done, trivially or tragically, many times every day. That is, we rush to credit – or is it blame – God for our opinion, our idea, our "revelation." "The Lord has given me a song," we announce, and those listening to our hideous wailing conclude that the song was probably one that he didn't want – a ripe pick for the "*Now that's what I call songs the Lord rejected*" or the "*WOW hits that didn't wow the Lord*" compilation albums. Little popes announce that "God has told them" to move house/marry Fred/take up knitting/leave the church/cover themselves in oil made in Israel and then march around the town carrying a bowl of oxtail soup. And the announcement that *The Lord has said* silences all dialogue because, well, the Lord has said. Leaders decide that God is on their side, and so anyone who dares to question their pontifications is labeled "divisive" or, worse, "rebellious," and the rest of the congregation is left wondering if they really ought to burn the dissenting witch. People rush to stab and wound leaders because they are "not the Lord's choice" (code for "well, we don't like him"). And churches divide: experts in conflict resolution agree that Christians can be among the worst at patching up their differences – because they insist on bringing God into the boxing ring as the One on their side, and on using his name to mandate their brutal sparring.

And of course, far more seriously, history has been smeared by the "God has surely told me" brigade, giving us the Crusades, the Inquisition and even an odd King Henry the Eighth, who was more than just a megalomaniac with a passing problem with chicken drumsticks – he went out of his way to use God and God's word to justify his serial womanizing. He employed theologians to burn the midnight oil to find a way he could use Leviticus to justify his divorce from Catherine of Aragon.

The abuse continues, as people drive airplanes into buildings and nations attack nations – and all in the name of their gods and God. The names of the gods change with the political weather, but the justifying goes on – and all to the glory of Allah, or Jesus, or freedom.

Perhaps it is insecurity that makes us rush to appeal to a heavenly stamp of approval for what we say and do. Perhaps we should listen a bit more to friends who can tell it to us straight, understanding that prophecy can only function in a loving crucible where awkward questions are asked as we seek to find the kernel of truth.

> **Perhaps it is insecurity that makes us rush to appeal to a heavenly stamp of approval for what we say and do**

God is on speaking terms with us – very much so. The ministry I am giving my life to, the house I live in and most of the major decisions that I have made over these last thirty years of faith – all of these have been forged in the place of hearing the God who is wonderfully interested enough to talk. But that realization – that God has said – comes at the end of what is sometimes an arduous journey. As we reflect, talk to friends, search Scripture, take long walks and perhaps pass up a few meals in order to pray, we are then able to confirm our sense that the whispers in our hearts and heads come from him. Rushing in where angels fear to tread only discredits the beautiful and vital gift of the prophetic, which then leads to disuse.

The church must hear the voice of God loud and clear. And the wider world needs to tune in too. We want the real thing – so let's take a little more time before we conclude, "God said."

ASHES INTO GOLD

Last week I met Larry and, at first, he fooled me. Larry reminds me of Clark Kent, also known as Superman, the master of disguise and superhuman on the side. Kent has an appearance of harmless domesticity, with his slicked-back hair and bespectacled eyes. But, come the cry of the damsel in distress, he pops into the nearest phone booth, slips into a rather gaudy outfit complete with blue tights, and flies off to save the world. All in a day's work. By day, no one knows what lurks beneath his nerdy exterior.

Larry has no penchant for brightly-colored hosiery, as far as I know, and he probably wouldn't be that useful if Lois Lane needed deliverance from an earthquake. Larry, in common with 99.9 per cent of the world's population, does not possess chiseled, movie star looks that would announce that he is "special." At first glance, he is just another ordinary chap. But he is, in reality, simply superhuman. Or so it seems.

Larry's daughter was murdered – strangled – in 1999. After the initial devastating news, there was further agony. For eight long months, the authorities were unable to identify any suspect in the killing. Larry and his family had already had to walk through the nightmare that every parent dreads. Late at night, when that teenager has not arrived safely home at the agreed hour, the imagination works overtime. What parent has not stared at the dark shadows of the bedroom ceiling, sweating

> **What parent has not stared at the dark shadows of the bedroom ceiling, sweating with fear at the thought that something tragic might have happened to their beloved child?**

with fear at the thought that something tragic might have happened to their beloved child? The sound of a telephone ringing in the small hours can set the pulse racing. Larry had received such a call: his lovely daughter was dead.

At first, he was consumed by a boiling anger: he wanted to commit murder himself and avenge his daughter. But then, very gradually, Larry began to sense a challenge from the God who knows the pain of a murdered Son: could he begin the long, arduous journey away from bitterness, towards that distant place of being able to forgive the as-yet-unknown person who had so brutally stolen his daughter's life?

It was a steep road to climb, but Larry resolved to make the trek, even though the pathway was beset by shadowy doubts. At first, he feared that he was betraying his daughter's memory by choosing to forgive. He realized that to truly offer forgiveness was in no way pardoning or excusing the criminal. Daily, Larry chose to continue his long climb up that hill of grace.

At last, a suspect was apprehended. And so Larry began to pray for justice – fearful that the man arrested might have been falsely accused, he prayed for the law enforcement authorities and the justice officials, asking God to give them insight and understanding. And then Larry began a new phase of prayer, asking that the murderer would discover the grace that Larry had found. He prayed that the killer might become a Christian.

Last week, five times over the course of a weekend, Larry came up onto the platform of our church and helped me to preach a sermon about forgiveness. More accurately, I helped him a little, because his words, ringing with pain and truth, echoed in people's hearts. People wept and wondered and struggled as he spoke with such clarity about his daily decision to forgive.

And here's what he said:

I will try to remember the events of Wednesday, April 28, 1999, the best I can. The day dawned so ordinarily; just another day. I was at work when the phone call that changed everything came. The caller identified himself as a detective from the Colorado Springs Police Department. My first thought was that my daughter, Lynette, was in trouble with the law or Social Services yet again. The detective asked me if I was the father of Lynette Fisher. I said that I was and then asked if there was a problem. He said that there was.

My mouth went very dry and my heart sank

The next comment from the policeman seemed to freeze my heart in a second. "I'm sorry to have to tell you that your daughter was found dead this morning." I couldn't believe what I was hearing. My mouth went very dry and my heart sank. I couldn't think of anything to say for a few seconds; it was as if time had stopped.

The policeman was gentle. "Are you still there?"

I quietly affirmed that I was and asked how this tragedy had happened. I began to think about my daughter's children and wanted to know if they were safe. He said that they were and began to tell me that Lynette had been murdered in the early hours of that morning. The weight of the world dropped upon me, and I found myself in gloomy darkness. I felt that I had been hit by a truck and was flat on my back. For a few minutes, I just did not know what to do. I knew that I had to get to Colorado Springs immediately. As the telephone conversation neared its end, I begin to fall apart. There was a great pain in my heart; my chest hurt badly. After I hung up the phone, I went to my work supervisor and told her what had happened. She took me into a conference room so that I could be alone, but I asked her to stay with me. I did not want to be alone at this time. I prayed.

Dear Father in Heaven,

Why did this have to happen to Lynette? Did I do something to bring this on her? I miss her so much! Why? Why? Please hold her for me. I know that she is with you!

Amen.

It was eight months before the police arrested anyone for the murder of my daughter. I was angry, but there was no one to direct my anger at. I felt so helpless and then I realized that I was powerless to do anything about her murder. Only God knew who the murderer was. I slowly realized that I was going to have to let Him take care of the situation. I admitted to God and a Christian friend that I was hurt, angry and wanted justice – but that there were defects in my own character that needed to be sorted out as well. With this realization I began to pray that God would remove these shortcomings, and so I made a list of people that I would harm if I did not give the situation over to God. The Holy Spirit helped me extend forgiveness to the man that had murdered my daughter and to myself. I did not know who this man was and this forgiveness in no way excuses the harm done against my daughter, her children and my family. But it was at this point that I placed this whole issue in His hands: great peace came.

Then on January 6, 2000, the Colorado Springs police told me that they had made an arrest in the murder of my daughter. I now had a new decision to make. I had to decide again to leave my daughter's death in God's hand or take it back. I began to take personal inventory and had to admit to God that I must leave this issue with Him. I remembered the peace that God had given me when I had given the problem to Him. I felt a great need to pray that the man the police had arrested was the correct man. I could not have lived with myself if there had been a case of mistaken identity, but I knew that God was in charge. God had me pray that the judge and jury would make the correct decision in this case. He even had me pray that my daughter's murderer would come to know Jesus.

The trial of Troy Williams began in January 2002 and was concluded towards the end of February. There were many bad things said about my daughter. I did not attend all the trial. Troy was sentenced to twenty-eight years with the possibility of parole after eight years. I know that God will have the final judgment in this case. At no time during the trial did Troy offer a statement to explain why he did what he did.

As far as I know, the killer has not yet made a decision to become a Christian. And his refusal to offer an explanation means that Larry is left with many, hauntingly unanswered, questions. Still he trusts.

Perhaps Larry isn't Superman after all: he is just another one of those regular humans who have discovered that grace, not kryptonite, is the transforming factor that gradually enables embittered, clawing people to unclench their fists and find true serenity. Larry is certainly testimony to the truth that the first person to benefit from the act of forgiveness is the one who forgives. He has determined to head towards

> **Larry is certainly testimony to the truth that the first person to benefit from the act of forgiveness is the one who forgives**

a brighter, more hope-filled horizon, rather than lingering, cowed down by bitterness, in a gloomy prison cell of rage. Larry chose to cling hard to God in his tragedy: and grace has turned his ashes into gold.

LYING IN LOVE

There are some well worn phases that scare me. When my fiendishly grinning dentist says, 'This will hurt a little', this usually means that he is going to attack my mouth with a hammer and chisel. When the airline pilot gently advises that the landing might be a little bumpy, he is preparing me for a roller coaster ride which might include me head butting the overhead baggage compartment while my breakfast revisits me. And when fellow Christians announce that they are about to 'speak the truth in love' to me, I'm tempted to head for the nearest nuclear fall-out shelter. Usually, when they murmur this indication of kindly torture to come, it means that they won't – speak the truth in love, that is. If they were, they wouldn't have to issue the health warning. Most of us have met the seriously spiritual person who has determined to cannibalise us verbally, but plans to do so in the nicest, most biblical way: all in the best possible taste. Let's face it: sadly we've all been that predator ourselves at times. Words easily become weapons of destruction, because of the power that they have to bruise. So we need to make hesitation a habit before putting our concerns into words and jumping headlong into conflict: silence and pause help us to respond rather than react. There are some small issues that can be left undiscussed, lest we become people who are always on safari to rebuke everybody about the tiniest detail. It's too easy, people of principle that we are, to become Pharisees who strain at gnats and swallow large camels, humps and fur and all. And of course, we do well to reflect rather than rush in, brain in neutral, mouth in fifth gear, because we might be wrong. Surprising as it seems to some, who seem to feel that the universe would explode if they ever made an error, there are times when we just get the wrong end of the stick and silence is indeed golden.

But I have been wondering recently about the tendency that we have to do the very opposite – and not speak the truth at all. Under the guise of Christian niceness, we end up agreeing with each other privately and then going elsewhere to broadcast our disagreements. We shake hands and hug and then, unwilling to be honest, retreat back into the shadows. This is called lying – in love. And there are some church situations where sadly, if you disagree and speak up, you will be quickly accused of being

> **We shake hands and hug and then, unwilling to be honest, retreat back into the shadows**

divisive (no, it's just that I have a brain and an opinion), rebellious (it's not that we want to stone you, just a little explanation would be helpful) or worst still the implication is that if we were just as deep as the real go-getters in the church, then we would surely understand. As it is, we must be blinded by our sad, fleshy immaturity, and when we advance a little, we will see the light like the rest of the spiritual goliaths around here. This is sometimes nothing less than full blown Gnosticism, where certain believers claimed that they had the edge on revelation and wisdom: insight had been given to them that the rest of the carnal plebs couldn't cope with. It is a control mechanism, and when used to silence a genuine enquiry or concern, it should be identified clearly for what it is: bunk. And if you think that I am pointing the finger exclusively at leaders and ministers here, you're wrong. They too have been devastated by that 'little spiritual group' in the church who seem to think that they are Olympic swimmers when the rest of us can only hope to sport width stripes (younger readers, in the 'old days', we got a little white cloth stripe to sew onto our trunks when we successfully swam a width of the swimming pool. I still wear mine with pride).

The call to be slow to speak and quick to listen is obviously a biblical one: but let's not get into pleasant unreality and think that we are honouring God as we do so. It is awkward and uncomfortable to have to push through to explore our differences and resolve our conflicts, but with God's help, we ought to be able to take that painful journey and still hold on to each other in fellowship and friendship. Let's be thoughtful, gracious, willing to give the benefit of the doubt – and real and authentic with it. And I say all that, to coin a phrase . . . in love.

> **The call to be slow to speak and quick to listen is obviously a biblical one**

HUMANS LIKE TO HERD

We humans like to run in herds. This well known fact has been especially demonstrated to me in Prague, the jewel of the Czech Republic, where I am speaking at the Salvation Army European Youth Congress. This magnificent medieval city is teeming with English tourists, many of whom are prepared to fork out cash for an airfare in exchange for cheap beer – the stag party scene is huge here. Boarding our flight at Bristol, we were greeted by a gaggle of giggling chaps sporting matching T-shirts, all embroidered with the name of their unfortunate friend and victim, who was wearing a skirt, red fish net tights and a shocking pink wig, which is called having fun. The group also had matching beer bellies, which is apparently deemed to be a desirable fashion item. I've been intrigued by the antics of a number of liquid lunch-imbibing Brits abroad here. Ladettes join in with raucous singing and celebrate the myth that following a certain football team makes one a superior human being – it's not a pretty sight, and as I watch the locals sniff with disdain, it's one that tempts me to resign from being British.

Superstitious religion feeds our herding instinct too

Prague has shown me once again that superstitious religion feeds our herding instinct too. In the centre of the beautiful Charles Bridge is an iconic statue which should be rubbed by all who pass by, or so local custom dictates. Lines of eager tourists wait their turn to give the brass a buffing, for reasons which are apparently unclear to most of them. The fact that everyone else is into pious polishing is enough. Next in line, please . . .

I fell victim to herding of the culinary kind, erroneously assuming that a full restaurant must indicate that good food is served there. Sampling the unfortunately described *Czech cuisine*, pork knuckle with sauerkraut and dumplings, was described by my wife Kay as 'a cultural experience', which is code for a cataclysmic disaster. The Czechs are generally quiet, undemonstrative people, which may be the result of their fondness for cabbage soup; one tends to be tight-lipped when battling with sudden outbreaks of internal combustion.

> As leaders of the largest Army in the world, the distinguished looking couple could have easily made a brief appearance

But today I saw a couple of refreshing jailbreaks from the herd. I have watched as the World Chief of the Salvationists General John Larsson and his wife Commissioner Freda have been hard at work here. As leaders of the largest Army in the world, the distinguished looking couple could have easily made a brief appearance that would have been the social equivalent of patting these eight hundred young people on the head, and then disappeared back to the elite seclusion often enjoyed by denominational big cheeses. Not these two. Over the last four days, they have laughed with and listened to hordes of grinning youth who could barely disguise their delight because their Head and First Lady are among them. This afternoon, in the sun baked Old Town Square, the General spoke at an open air gathering with warmth, compassion, and sterling clarity about the Lord Jesus. A few moist eyes were evident among the tourist crowd during the event, and the Army youth cheered their silver-haired hero on.

And I watched with greater fascination as a young, trendy looking Salvationist chap broke away from the safe camaraderie of his fellow Christians and made his way into a large group of shirtless, lager-loaded chaps who had more than their fair share of tattoos – and who were quite happy, so to speak. He smiled at and shook hands with each of the men, and chatted warmly about God and life for a good half hour, answering their loud, slurred questions with kindness. When it came time to bid them farewell, it was obvious that he had made a real impression. Strangely, as he walked away, it was as if suddenly his audience reverted to herding; they burst into a loud, mocking song, as if they were embarrassed at the vulnerability that they had shared with brave young man. Who knows what long term impact his words and smile might have?

As I left the square, the sound of drunken soccer songs once again in the air, I wanted to raise my hat to the leaders and troops of the Salvation Army. Many of them wear uniform – but helpfully, those I've met this weekend aren't given to mindless uniformity.

And I'm wondering about my own herding instincts. Sometimes, going with the flow just won't work, especially if the flow is headed over Niagara. Will someone – perhaps me – please just stand up and be counted?

THE PERILS OF MACHINES

Where would I be without Brenda? She is in her mid-thirties, has the shrill voice of a permanently irritated headmistress, and we are now having a relationship. Brenda is a source of special comfort to me late at night when I am driving alone – she has a doctorate in geography. Specifically, she has committed every street, road, lane and motorway in Britain to memory. She is the voice inside my GPS system, and she is my deliverer, since I have a special gift for getting lost – all over the world. My only criticism is that she seems emotionally repressed. I'd like her to clap, cheer and offer warm congratulations when I arrive somewhere, but her flat, monotone voice just coldly announces that I have now reached my destination and says nothing more. Of course, "she" is just a robot. I don't introduce her to my friends.

Brenda is just one of many machines that now surround me. My palm pilot (I haven't given the palm a name yet – what do you think I am, mad?) tells me what to do each day, as well as providing the telephone numbers of everyone I've met since birth. And Larry the . . . I mean my *laptop*, allows me to check the size of my overdraft, receive three hundred emails daily and write this article while I'm being driven down the highway.

But my marriages to my machines have not been entirely happy. I've bought a stack of devices that were supposed to save me time, but I haven't found the time to

> I've bought a stack of devices that were supposed to save me time, but I haven't found the time to read the instructions

read the instructions. I accidentally poured the contents of a boiling kettle into my laptop, which literally screamed and gave up the ghost, taking a million vital details of my life to a hot watery grave. And, through a series of thoughtless key strokes, I managed to format the hard drive on another computer. For those readers unfamiliar with this jargon, this is the hi-tech equivalent of opening the top of one's head, removing one's brain and lobbing it into a trash can. The computer was stunned when I told it to kill itself. "Are you sure?" it pleaded. Presumably brainless myself, I told it that yes, I was certain. Goodbye to another five years of diaries, accounts, sermons and everything. When I realized what I had done, I was a little perturbed – if being a little perturbed means running around the house screaming like a banshee.

But there is another, more subtle, peril in being hemmed in by my electrical friends. These machines all exist in my life for one sole purpose – to serve me. They live and hum only for my comfort, efficiency, information and direction. I give them nothing except input so that they will serve me better. They are metal appendages that are bolted on to me solely to improve my lot; I am their lord. And when they become obsolete – which seems to happen about thirty minutes after I have purchased them – I will forsake them without a thought or a shed

People can become mere things that we embrace or reject according to their ability to serve us

tear for a flashier, but equally temporary, gizmo.

The danger of all of this is that I can start to treat the people around me in the same way. Failing to see beyond the horizon of my own selfish wants and needs, I begin to view my marriage, my friendships and "my" church all as entities that exist primarily for my benefit. People can become mere things that we embrace or reject according to their ability to serve us. How many human beings have I encountered today without ever really seeing *them?* Those who spend their lives meeting people are particularly prone to this: the hospital doctor who refers to "the broken leg in bed 5" has lost sight of the person and only sees an ailment to cure. Insisting that we refer to people with disabilities appropriately is about far more than using politically correct language – it is honoring the basic right that we all share to be viewed as fully human.

But I have learned a useful lesson from my machines, too. When shutting my computer down, I methodically close all the various programs I've used, one by one. I'm learning to do something similar with my mind, especially when I'm about to meet people. If my brain is cluttered with the debris of too many mental journeys, then I will fail to focus and give my fullest attention to those I meet – they will just be one of many "windows" that I am keeping open. We can give others the wondrous gift of our fullest attention; to do so confirms the truth that each one of us is a unique, fascinating creation, worth more than a passing glance. Someone recently told me about how God used me to help them come to faith at a Christian conference. I wondered which sermon it was, but my speculations were wrong. Apparently this person came up to me as I was walking to a seminar, and I slowed down and chatted. My willingness to pause was sufficiently impressive to bring them to a decision about Christ. I share this without a hint of smugness; I'm painfully aware that there have probably been too many times when my hurry meant that I was insensitive and unwilling to be interrupted. On this occasion, by God's grace, I got it right.

Meanwhile, back in the fast lane on the highway, Brenda is telling me that I have worked so hard today, that she's very proud of me, that I should stop for a coffee. I wish.

R.S.V.P.

It was the moment that I both loved and dreaded. The sermon had ended, the speaker's Bible had been closed – and now it was time for the congregation to do their bit. Invariably, I used to be one of the first people to respond.

This part of the service is called by a variety of names, according to your tribe and tradition: some dub it the "altar call," others the "response" or "ministry time." And of course some churches don't have this at all, ever – while others don't consider that they've had a kosher Christian meeting without a pause for open response at the end. Some churches provide gentle background music, while others stoically respond in stern silence. Sometimes the respondent is only required to raise a hand or stand for prayer – and there are, of course, the Billy Graham style come-down-to-the-front-*now* shuffling moments, too. Salvationists have their "penitents' benches," and I've visited pentecostal churches in America that have wooden "altars" with built-in tissue dispensers conveniently provided for the tearful.

> I've visited pentecostal churches in America that have wooden "altars" with built-in tissue dispensers conveniently provided for the tearful

Like anything else in church life, these so-called altar calls can be abused and manipulated, or they can become yet another empty ritual that is more about affirming that the speaker has said something useful than about anything more deeply significant. *(Result! Loads of people came forward!)* And some "altar calls" insult one's intelligence, particularly when the speaker begins by asking for volunteers for martyrdom, but, seeing few takers, ends up by giving the impression that you should be at the front, *right now*, if you've ever eaten breakfast at some time in your life. I also fear the *Nescafe* spirituality that can result from being told that, whatever the issue, it will be taken care of, instantly, if you'll only take a quick stroll in the direction of the pulpit.

But, for the most part, these can be positive times. We are in the church, which is a community where we constantly make choices to align our lives with Jesus – and where some prayerful support from those around us is helpful.

In my Christian youth, I responded to these appeals at every opportunity. I was rabidly desperate to please God, and I would rush forward to respond at the end of any and every sermon, regardless of the content. I was surely every preacher's dream, ever ready as I was to make a quick dash in yet another flush of recommitment. Sometimes my response bore no relationship to any kind of reality. If the preacher had asked for any Taiwanese dyslexic basket weavers in the house to go forward for prayer, I would have been found at the front, ready for a career in wicker. A call for volunteers to lead the local "Women's Aglow" chapter would have found me eagerly front-bound, offering my piloting skills to those flaming sisters.

But one common factor stands out from my spiritual sprinting down a hundred naves and aisles – almost invariably, I went forward to *apologize.* Like a whipped puppy flinching because of the expectation of yet another slap, I assumed that God would only ever have words of critique and complaint to shout at arch-sinner Lucas. The possibility that he might want to encourage, strengthen, or simply let me know that I was doing okay never occurred to me. Ever.

And so I repented of a few things that weren't actually sin. One sunny evening I went forward to apologize to God for feeling happy, as if a feeling of anything less than pure *joy* was unworthy. I also went forward to repent of my feelings towards Kay – now my wife. Surely, I reasoned, it could not possibly be God's will that I marry her – after all, I fancied . . . er, I mean I found her attractive. Having been schooled in the view that God's beautiful plan for my life would probably be precisely the opposite of anything that I might like, I deduced that I'd have to marry someone really ugly. No prizes for the bright spark who surmises that Kay also believed this somewhat warped idea.

I've just finished a lengthy study of the seven churches of Revelation, and I was stunned to discover that Jesus had *no* word of rebuke at all for two of them – only commendation and a verbal pat on the back. The lack of rebuke is . . . stunning. Why are we at home with the threat of judgment, but struggle with the idea that God might want to tell us that we're doing alright?

Perhaps there's a big surprise waiting for us when we finally step forward on the last day, when we see Jesus face-to-face. Is it possible that it won't be heaven itself that leaves us breathless – that it won't be the megaton singing of exuberant angelic choirs that blows us away on that day, or the first sightseeing of a new city where the Lamb will be our light? Perhaps the hugest shock of all will be the sight of a perfect God, whispering the most unexpected greeting to plebs like us:"well done, good and faithful servant."

THE GATEKEEPER

She glared at me with cold, dark eyes, undisguised contempt etched across her scowling face. "Did *you* leave the front gate open?" she demanded, her finger pointing my way accusingly. I flushed crimson, the guilty one. I'd been caught red-handed by my next-door neighbor. Our apartments share the same entrance gate and, while I was loading my car, I had committed the cardinal sin of leaving the iron gate ajar for a good two minutes. This was my first interaction with the irate lady and, the way our happy little chat was going, it didn't look like she'd want to join our upcoming Alpha course. In fact, it didn't look like I was going to live. I stammered out my apology, which was not enough. She treated me to a lecture about how gates should be shut at all times, save for a few seconds when people had to pass through them. I apologized again and fled indoors, a shamed criminal.

Within minutes I had built up an enraged head of steam. How dare she talk to me like that! I tried to pray, but I could only get as far as "Oh Lord, kindly smite her with festering boils, a bolt of lightning, or perhaps a few million frogs," which didn't seem quite right. After all, some of the frogs might wander into *our* flat. I tried to read the Bible, but unfortunately found one of those "Lord, break the teeth of my enemies" Psalms and suddenly had a picture of me jumping up and down on her dentures. Not helpful.

> **Within minutes I had built up an enraged head of steam**

Perhaps a stiffly-worded letter, one of those "I have rights and don't you jolly well forget it," would do the trick. And then, for a moment, my enraged fantasies got the better of me. Perhaps I *should* send her an invite to the Alpha course, delivered through her window, wrapped around a brick. (Don't call the police or, worse, write to the publisher – the moment passed quickly.)

I decided to go and knock on her door and announce, kindly but firmly, that I was an adult and would like to be treated as such in the future. Helpfully, my wife Kay is supernaturally patient. She has completed one of the most intensive courses in character development available: twenty-six years of marriage to me. She is also wise and knew that I would err more on being firm than kind. "Leave it," she said. So I did. She didn't.

Over the last few months Kay has embarked on a mission to be kind to our unfriendly gatekeeper next door. She has smiled at her, waved, chatted about the weather, opened her heart and shut the gate. A remarkable change has occurred. A few weeks ago, there was a knock on our door. It was our lady of the gate, smiling. I thought the universe was going to explode. Kay had mentioned that we were having some building work done, but that we'd be away in America when the workmen were due to arrive. Now our grinning neighbor was offering to look after the key and keep an eye on things while we were gone.

Recently, we decided to take a little gift to her by way of appreciation. And for thirty minutes she tearfully told us about her long-term battle with depression (which is keeping her off work), and about the grief that is hers due to an avalanche of tragedy that has nearly buried her and her

> She tearfully thanked us for our gift and seemed genuinely desperate for our friendship

husband of late. She tearfully thanked us for our gift and seemed genuinely desperate for our friendship.

Just a few days ago, Kay invited our neighbor over for a cup of tea. Their hour of conversation included a few more tears. Kay offered her one of my books, which she took gladly, promising that both she and her husband would read it. Who knows where all of this will lead?

And now, as I reflect, I thank God that I did not hammer on her door and protest my rights. I realize that hurt people hurt people, and that a frosty glare, a rude, brusque comment or an unpleasant demeanor may hide a world of pain. My "entirely justified" irritation might well have sent that drowning women under for good. I suddenly understood the gate episode. Small things matter when you live with 24/7 sadness.

I also learned that showing grace isn't complex rocket science. Kay had taught me (once again) that the habit of mugging people with kindness is a winning way.

And I'm praying that God will help me to respond rather than react when others irritate and wound me, and to keep my mouth shut. And the gate shut, too.

ARTHUR

Arthur smelled very bad.

No one really knew where he came from, but our wrinkled noses certainly told us when he was coming. He always wore the same grubby, threadbare overcoat, his teeth were impossibly crooked and he was famous – or infamous – for disturbing our Sunday services.

Arthur was very strange indeed, and for years we couldn't work out why, though there was plenty of speculation. Some thought that he had systematically simmered his brains in alcohol. Others guessed that some unspeakable tragedy had befallen him in younger years, catapulting him into a mental illness from which he had never recovered. "He's not all there" was the somewhat politically incorrect popular diagnosis. One or two demon hunters muttered that there were definitely devils to deal with. And some of us thought that Arthur was just a wild old eccentric from London's East End who liked to have a good laugh at the world and didn't care about those who preferred to not join in the fun.

Arthur would usually interrupt the preacher, asking an off-the-wall question that a) was right in the middle of the sermon, and b) had no relevance to what was being talked about. A message on prayer would be punctuated by an enquiry concerning how likely it might be that Queens Park Rangers soccer team would win next Saturday's match and what the actual score would be. A study on the High Priest in Hebrews would prompt a public interrogation about the

A study on the High Priest in Hebrews would prompt a public interrogation about the rising price of haddock in the supermarkets

rising price of haddock in the supermarkets. Firmly, but with incredible kindness, our lovely, patient pastor would ask Arthur to be quiet and tell him that he'd love to pick up the chat about soccer or seafood at the end of the service. Arthur would always grunt the same apology and settle down for a while, until the next urgent question popped into his brain and prompted another outburst. We eventually got used to it, although it was a nightmare for visiting preachers who had not been forewarned.

Once our church rented a bus and we all attended a district event in another town. Arthur came along and brought his dog with him. The service was conducted by a well-spoken, mildly pompous minister who had no knowledge of Arthur's questioning habits. Those were the days when we used to "sing choruses" rather than have a time of worship and, appallingly, we were also invited to shout out our requests for the next song – a kind of devotional desert island discs. At the end of a rather dreary song, the minister asked the packed church if they had any requests. Arthur put his hand up. The immaculately-suited minister stared down through the gold-rimmed glasses perched on the end of his nose at the scruffy man in the crowd, noted the dog at his side and said, "Yes, brother?"

"Can you change these awful chairs? They're really 'ard, and my bum's killing me"

"I have a request," chortled Arthur, a huge grin taking over his entire face.

"Delightful. Lovely. What is your request?" asked the minister.

"Can you change these awful chairs? They're really 'ard, and my bum's killing me. Even me dog 'ates 'em."

Blood drained from the pastor's face. He had probably never heard the word "bum," and possibly didn't even possess one. I looked across the congregation. Shoulders were shaking in barely controlled mirth; many were trying desperately to avoid laughing out loud. It was truly wonderful, and it brought a bit of planet earth to what had become a somewhat ethereal evening.

Of course there were the unfunny times, too, when visitors would come to our church and be intimidated by Arthur's antics. One very rich, fur-coated lady, for example, decided to attend our Sunday morning service – and, sadly, got seated right behind Arthur.

Halfway through the sermon, he turned around to her, smiled and whispered, "Psssst. Lady . . . are you 'ot?"

She snuggled deeper into her dead animal and replied that, no, thank you, she was not hot. She was comfortable. He turned back and faced the front.

Two minutes later the interrogation began again. "Pssst . . . you. Are you 'ot?" Once again the now concerned lady affirmed that the temperature was just fine for her, thank you very much. Arthur turned back again.

The third time, the question was greeted by a more frosty response. "Are you 'ot?" Arthur demanded. "Yes I am quite hot," the now flushed lady muttered, hoping to end the discussion by confessing that she was actually sweating – which, by now, she was.

"Well you'll be 'otter in 'ell," Arthur said with a huge smile and not an ounce of malice. Sadly, but not surprisingly, we never saw the fur-clad lady again.

Then one day the mystery of Arthur's mild madness was solved. It turned out that he had been the innocent victim of an East End gang war many years earlier, in his younger days. A revenge attack – probably over territory – went badly wrong with a mix-up over addresses. Two hired thugs knocked on Arthur's door and then knocked him over the head with an iron bar, creating some catastrophic and irreversible brain damage. Arthur was never the same. In classic East End style, when the gangsters realized that they had attacked the wrong man, they came back, apologized and helped him get to the hospital.

Arthur recovered – but the essential skills of tact and appropriateness were gone forever. For the rest of his life, he just said whatever came into his damaged head.

Arthur is probably long gone now. I'm certain that he is not interrupting Jesus right now in heaven, since he will have gotten his full faculties back – and a whole lot more besides. But I'm so glad that he was a part of our church. Arthur didn't really fit anywhere else, and he had been handed a life sentence of being odd and strange because of his calamity. His idiosyncrasy gave us the opportunity to be kind, compassionate and inclusive. He reminded us that the church is not a trophy case crammed with nice, together people. It's a place where those tragically dubbed as misfits can find that they fit, where odd types can belong and believe.

Which is good news for us all. Arthur's malady was, at times, painfully obvious: we hide our dents and disabilities more efficiently. But there should be a welcome for us all – a welcome of which we are all a part.

CARELESS WHISPERS

Cordless radio microphones are all the rage these days in churches. Personally I hate them. For one thing, they require me to secrete the connecting cable somewhere about my being, and often the sound technician insists on helping. This means that suddenly I have a complete stranger ferreting around in my underwear – and all in the name of science. And the problems don't end here. These radio mikes go through batteries like Popeye with spinach, which means that one can be cut off in one's prime and rendered silent while still mouthing words. This has happened to me more than once: one clueless brother didn't realize what was happening and thanked me for my powerful ministry in mime. Another gave his hearing aid a violent slap and almost knocked himself unconscious.

But surely the main challenge with the unobtrusive radio mike is that people often forget that they are wearing it and therefore fail to switch it off. This is excruciating if you speak, invite people forward for prayer and then pray with them while the broadcasting device is still switched on. Suddenly Mavis' urgent petition concerning her husband's chronic erectile dysfunction becomes a matter of bemused fascination among the whole congregation, as her tearful prayer request booms through the loudspeakers.

The radio microphone also means that the preacher's attempts at singing during worship are often shared at earsplitting volume with all

The radio microphone also means that the preacher's attempts at singing during worship are often shared at earsplitting volume with all – which is most unfortunate, particularly if the preacher is good with sermons but makes a noise like that of a ferret being slowly strangled when attempting melody. There's nothing worse than the sound of a church singing in the key of G while the preacher subjects any listening angels to agony as he or she drones on in the key of H. (I know, there is no key of H. That's my point.)

And they should teach ministers in training something about microphone etiquette when using the lavatory facilities. Another friend reports being live, as it were, when he slipped into the bathroom. Unaware that his radio microphone was still switched on, within seconds the church that he led was far more intimately acquainted with him than they could have ever wished for. A few nervous souls fled the building, fearing that the thunder storm that had suddenly erupted might get worse. So now I reach for that *off* button automatically. There are some conversations that I want to keep private, which can be appropriate.

But I've also been challenged recently about the fact that there are times when I'd like to reach for the little black button and make sure that *God* doesn't hear what comes out of my mouth. Sometimes we abuse the intimacy that we enjoy with close friends by subconsciously giving each other permission to use language and humor that would shame us if the conversation were broadcast in public. While I want to be able to relax and be intimate with a few people, and enjoy a level of sharing and vulnerability that might be inappropriate for crowd consumption, I don't want to be one who creates a permissive atmosphere around those I love – for their sake, or for mine.

No black button (switching off God's ability to hear us) actually exists. Without painting him as the sentry in the sky, he calls us to be responsible for the words that we allow to pass our lips. Our words can so easily bruise,

> **No black button (switching off God's ability to hear us) actually exists**

maim, malign and destroy – or bless, encourage and bring life. We will be called to account for the way that we've used or abused the gift of speech: "But I tell you that men will have to give account on the day of judgment for every careless word they have spoken" (Matt. 12:36).

In the meantime, I'll practice care around radio mikes. A friend reports that he reluctantly officiated at a wedding where he didn't have confidence that the union would last. He then left the mike on as he and a colleague proceeded down the aisle following the happy couple's exchange of vows. Thinking that his comment would be private, he muttered, "I'll give this one six months," to his fellow clergyman, which drew a congregational gasp from the gathered relatives. They gave him a hostile reception at the reception.

Ouch.

FATHER OF THE BRIDE

We sat there, two big tall men, a pathetic pair, and just sobbed our hearts out. The reason for this unbridled outpouring of grief was Steve Martin's warm and poignant film, *Father of the Bride*. Chris and I, both fathers of beautiful twelve-year-old daughters, were suddenly and overwhelmingly appalled by the reality that our girls would very likely fall in love and leave us one day. The very thought of it made us feel quite bereft. There was nothing else for it. Our daughters were both sleeping – as were the rest of our vacationing households. We went to their rooms, woke them up and insisted that they come and sit with us and talk for a while. After all, soon they'd be thirteen, and not a precious second should be wasted. They sat on our laps and rolled their eyes at each other, amazed by their sad, blubbering dads. Love always brings tears of some kind.

Nine years later, I fought to keep my eyes dry again as I listened to Ben, my son-in-law for all of two hours, give his bridegroom's speech. He had proposed by taking Kelly to the Alps in Switzerland. He asked for her hand in marriage – and then the pair of them parachuted off the side of the mountain to symbolize the beginning of the adventure that would be their lives entwined together.

> He asked for her hand in marriage – and then the pair of them parachuted off the side of the mountain

Their wedding day had been everything that we could have hoped for – and more. The chilly December day had been remarkably kissed by sunshine, which seemed to echo the warmth in our hearts: our daughter Kelly had found a very good man indeed as a partner for life. And then it was time for Kelly to give her speech. She had determined not to be the silent and blushing bride, and she wanted to make her own verbal contribution to the day. She spoke with warmth and wit, and then she said something that stopped me dead in my tracks.

"Some of you know my dad because of his writing, or you've heard him speak somewhere. You may be wondering what he's really like behind the scenes. I'm here to tell you."

Nervous giggles ensued, and many eyes fastened on my increasingly crimsoned face. I was tempted to rush out of the building, never to be seen again, and become a missionary to some far-flung tribe. Undeterred, Kelly continued.

"I want to say that dad has always tried to live out what he preaches. What you see is what you get. I love you, Dad."

Time for the waterworks again.

A few more delightful hours later, it was time for the bride and groom to leave. In *Father of the Bride*, there is much chaos at this point of the day. The beloved daughter leaves her reception without being able to bid her exhausted and emotional wreck of a father goodbye.

Everyone lined up to form a huge archway through which Kelly and Ben would run. The only question for me was, where was Kelly? I knew that she would emerge from the arch and get straight into the waiting car – and I wanted to be sure to hug and kiss her goodbye before that moment. Suddenly, I got a message – Jeff, Kelly's looking for you – she wants to say goodbye before she runs through the arch. Meet her at the front door now . . .

As I took my beautiful daughter into my arms, she held me close and whispered, "Dad, it's just like *Father of the*

Bride. Remember, on holiday, all those years ago? And like Steve Martin, we nearly missed our goodbye."

The car drove off, and joy swept over my aching heart: a new life for her with Ben was beginning. But Kelly's speech was the most priceless parting gift, not least because it helped me to remember what really matters.

Looking back on my days as a dad, I am so aware that there were so many mistakes – some of which torment me. In the heat of too many moments, I spoke words that I wish I could take back. And certainly I wish I'd cancelled that preaching tour, or that appointment at the church, and just played some more

> I certainly missed too many other priceless moments – and all in the name of ministry

with my children. I didn't miss our wedding day goodbye, but I certainly missed too many other priceless moments – and all in the name of ministry. I also look back with gratitude and thanksgiving. There were no training sessions for parenting back then. My daughter's words of affirmation were a great gift to me that day.

Ministry has meant that there have been many roles I've fulfilled. But none of them comes close to the privilege of being father to the bride.

A CONFUSED FOREIGNER

I had eagerly anticipated our trip to France, but I had not prepared for it very well. I have no language skills other than English, except for just one sentence in French learned back in high school: "Excuse me, how do I get to the railway station?" Sadly, I have never yet needed to actually get to a station while in France. And, in the unlikely event that I might need to know the way, I wouldn't understand the directions anyway, as they would be, well, in French.

I had not even consulted a phrase book prior to this latest trip, an essential little item for swanning around in foreign parts. My previous attempts at communicating, phrase book in hand, had led to disaster when I got my pronunciation wrong. Under the influence of my masterly French pronunciation, the words for "chair" and "dog" sound surprisingly similar (which just goes to prove my point about my linguistic finesse). And so I asked a café owner if I might perch on one of her domestic pets. She gave me a look that needed no interpretation – it was the internationally understood grimace reserved for the criminally insane.

So now I am one of those sad British tourists who speaks English with a French accent when in France – as if that would impress anyone.

Jeff: *(entering bakery)* "'Ello, 'ow are yoooo, mon-sewer?"

Shop owner: "Pardon?"

Jeff: "I am indeed exceeding grateful to be in your delicissimo shop, in pursuit as I am of the croissant for myself and the bambinos" (at this point I obviously thought I was in Italy rather than France).

Shop owner: "Pardon?"

Jeff: "Four of those *siv vous plais*" (pointing to the croissants).

Shop owner: "Certainly. I'm from Grimsby. Moved here to France last year. Can I get you anything else today? Mushy peas?"

Jeff, blushing, exits shop and sprints away at speed.

But this was just the beginning of our sorrows. Our moment of real, red-faced agony came as we stood admiring a beautiful church building; a soft, candlelit glow warmed the ancient stained glassed windows. Suddenly a gleaming black, chauffeur-driven limousine pulled up alongside its ancient oak doors.

"Wow! A French wedding! I've got to catch this on video!" exclaimed Chris, my best friend and eager documenter of overseas nuptials. He proceeded to haul the largest camera I have ever seen up onto his shoulder. Those were the days when "portable" and "video" were words that didn't fit into the same sentence. Like early mobile phones, which usually required a jeep to haul them around, so primitive video cameras looked big enough for a newsroom. We cheered and clapped and waved, eager to see the blushing bride. And then we became the blushing spectators as we realized that the man with the black top hat was not the best man, but a somber faced undertaker. Understandably, he looked quite bewildered by our cheerleading greeting for the corpse. He marched stiffly but quickly to the back door of the limo, revealing an elegant walnut coffin. Throwing confetti didn't seem appropriate. For the second time that day I found myself fleeing in embarrassment, this time with the rest of the crowd in tow, Chris puffing and panting under the weight of his outside broadcast unit.

And over a cup of very strong coffee (espresso – not what we ordered, but what we got) we licked our wounds, held two minutes' silence out of respect for the dead and pondered the difficulties of being in a strange country. It was all so disorientating – with a language we couldn't fathom, brides that weren't and chairs that barked if you sat on them.

And I wondered . . . are some of our churches as bewildering to visitors? It's difficult enough to walk into a building that houses a group of people that mostly know each other, some for many years. That alone can make you feel like the stranger at a family party, without even an assurance that your invitation is genuine. But then, some of our churchy customs and vocabulary can also make the newcomer feel even more like an intruder who should hotfoot it away at the earliest opportunity.

Is the Christian subculture like a foreign land to many? I wondered what guests would think of the minister's smiling announcement at a charismatic church I attended recently. Eager to encourage the use of the gifts of the Spirit, he didn't stop to think about how *very* strange his choice of words was.

"Does anyone here have a tongue? Stand up now, and share it with us all."

It got ever stranger – at least in the eyes of the uninitiated. Anxious to see someone offer some words of testimony, he delivered another bizarre exhortation.

"Would someone like to come up here and share their heart?" Guests might have been mystified: churches are occasionally used as blood transfusion centers, but a public appeal for transplant organ donors was surely pushing it. Another church leader helpfully "shed some light" on what his local church was about:

"If we're all connected in spirit to the vision, then we'll see a breakthrough in the heavenlies – but it won't come without much groaning. We've just got to push through, and dig in for the long haul, and we'll see the rising tide. Is that clear?"

Those who knew nodded that they did indeed know. Those who weren't sure also nodded, *pretending* that they knew. And those who hadn't got the first clue scratched their heads, ducked and privately wondered if the inmates had taken over the asylum.

And "radical" and more creative churches: beware. Very strange things can happen when there is an unexplained emphasis on spiritual warfare in a local congregation. Perhaps we shouldn't be surprised if visitors are stunned when that prophetic chap, dressed up as Braveheart (his face daubed with red and blue war paint) enriches the Sunday morning service by slapping the living daylights out of an upturned oil drum. In some churches, one of the most radical things that could occur would be the offering of some *predictability*. Now that really would be different.

But even more traditional churches can be confusing to outsiders, especially when it's assumed that everyone knows when to sit down, when to stand and when to kneel. Even precious songs that pulsate with meaning for us can bewilder. I remember the first time I heard the beautiful words of Wesley's hymn:

> There is a fountain filled with blood
> Drawn from Emmanuel's veins
> And sinners plunged beneath that flood
> Lose all their guilty stains

I was stunned. This sounded like something out of a low-budget Hammer horror movie. Let's not lose the hymn; but let's take time to do a little explaining lest our guests fear that they have wandered onto the set of a Transylvanian castle.

And being sensitive to guests who visit our churches goes beyond giving a few words of explanation and thinking through our choice of language. It means that we don't look surprised when they unthinkingly try to light up a cigarette during

It means that we don't look surprised when they unthinkingly try to light up a cigarette during third hymn

the third hymn, swear during an after-service conversation, or wear a miniskirt that falls just beneath the chin to a church social event. It surely means going out of our way to offer a few warm words of welcome – and being ready to be faithful tour guides for their potentially bewildering excursion around Planet Church.

Meanwhile, back in France, the café owner's dog has just shown up, and he is staring intently at us Brits. He looks nervous.

FALSE ASSUMPTIONS

It had been the most wonderful family holiday on the Oregon coast. We played our way through long, balmy days, crabbing off the pier and tugging at kites on an almost windless beach. The sunsets saw us gathered around campfires, roasting marshmallows. One night, our daughter Kelly asked if we could sleep outside by the campfire. I was thrilled at the idea; our borrowed caravan was tiny and climbing into bed demanded that I fold myself in half. Restful sleep had eluded me, as I discovered what a fiver feels like in a wallet. Sleeping out by the glowing embers was a fine proposal.

Just as she was drifting off to sleep, Kelly asked for some assurance. "Daddy . . . there aren't any snakes around here, are there?" I laughed and assured her that there would definitely not be any reptilian

The fact that my words were absurd did not occur to me

visitors. After all, this was a state park – and they wouldn't allow snakes in the park, now would they? The fact that my words were absurd did not occur to me. I believed myself. Did I think that any passing rattlesnake would bump into a large sign that yelled: "State Park: No Snakes Allowed," whereupon it would sigh ruefully and slither off in another direction? I drifted off to sleep, satisfied in my delusion and blissfully unaware of an unfortunate fact. I had parked my camp bed over a snake nest.

Seven hours later, my eyelids opened. I smiled at the blue sky above and rolled over, only to find myself staring down a mere nine inches at no less than three snakes. People throughout the park could hear my screaming and shouting. I think I yelled "Hosanna!" Or something like that.

I had lulled my daughter – and myself – to sleep with a totally false assumption; my comforting words were not based in truth. Thankfully no harm was done (except that poor Kelly was rudely awakened by a parental banshee). Sadly, it's all too easy to meander through life, believing absurdities – and then be surprised and disappointed when our cherished ideas turn out to be drivel. Many of us have a collection of misunderstandings: prayer should be easy; Bible study is always fascinating; only other people get cancer; church should cater to me and my preferences; deep down we are good people and so will never do anything especially terrible; our leaders are nearly perfect; our leaders are secret Satanists; our church is the best in town; and my holiday destination will look something like the photo in the brochures.

Other common misconceptions include the following: God's will for your life will always be rather horrid ("Never say that you don't want to be a missionary – God will hear and call you to the last place you'd want to go.") –

> **It is possible to eat a Chicken Vindaloo without a subsequent gastric affliction**

or, conversely, that whatever it is you happen to want to do must also be God's will for your life; when life is good, God is good (what is he when life is awful?); all non-Christians are nasty; it's always someone else's turn to buy the drinks; it is possible to eat a Chicken Vindaloo without a subsequent gastric affliction; all charismatics are mad; and all conservative evangelicals are boring sad types who wear bicycle clips in bed.

Only last night I heard about a Christian who prayed that one of his relatives would be spared from the terminal illness that struck him. The loved one died – and now, not only has he abandoned his faith, but he has become an angry, aggressive opponent of all things Christian. God does seem to intervene with miraculous healing at times, but this person has no right to act as if he can tell God what to do and when; his faith was placed in a misapprehension rather than a reality. That is one of the chief reasons we need to be thoroughly grounded and immersed in Scripture, lest our faith be a patchwork quilt of vague hopes, catchy slogans and the collective "wisdom" of some of those extreme television preachers who really ought to take up prison ministry in Alcatraz – now that it's deserted. Three times Paul warned his young friend Timothy to stay away from "myths and old wives' tales" – which is sound advice, if a little hard on elderly married storytellers.

Let's work harder at developing an informed, biblically-founded faith. Let's read our Bibles more; pray for discernment; use the brains God gave us; think of others before ourselves; let God be God. We can all sleep soundly and face another day without succumbing to despair because we have a hope that is sure.

And be careful where you park your camp bed.

FIRST IMPRESSIONS

Shalom.

My knowledge of Hebrew is somewhat limited – *Shalom* is the only word that I can say here in Israel with confidence, although I am wrestling with a temptation to shout "Oy!" at the end of every sentence. Only in this bizarre, wonderful and hugely confusing country would you see a sign banning unauthorized communion taking – a picture of bread and wine in a circle with a line drawn through it, in the style of a no smoking warning. The authorities are obviously worried about tourists slipping off for a crafty time of sacramental fellowship on "holy" sites without "proper" leadership, so in some places it's declared illegal. Imagine the police stopping a dodgy-looking pilgrim: "Freeze – hands up! We don't want any trouble – just be a good boy and hand over the loaf and the Merlot . . ."

There is, of course, a vast array of religious kitsch available. Here you can buy your very own crown of thorns (certificate of authenticity included) or bottled water from the River Jordan (green and slimy, but apparently rather holy, H_2O).

There are also endless spots where epic stuff apparently happened. Helpfully we have been assisted by Smulich, a marvelous guide who has never once even nudged us towards revering the place where Moses allegedly stopped for a coffee.

But the warning most inconsistent with the spirit of the place was posted at the beach where tradition says Jesus cooked breakfast for weary, hungry Peter and his pals – the event described in the twenty-first chapter of John's Gospel. As we strolled up to the entrance gate, yet another sign screamed a warning in forbidding red lettering:

"Holy place. No shorts."

Rats. I was the only member of our group wearing this item of clothing that God apparently doesn't like. Since they came

"Holy place. No shorts"

almost down to my knees I hoped for a grace dispensation, but I was stopped at the gate by a stern-looking chap who remonstrated with me because my knees were in view. In the end he let me in, but only after I promised that, if I met the priest who guarded the beach (obviously an "attack" priest on the lookout for knee-flashing communicants), I would say that I had been duly warned at the gate. I was then instructed to pull my shorts as far down over my apparently lust-inducing knees as possible – which I did. But there were fresh dangers afoot. This adjustment seriously inhibited my ability to walk, so the prospect of tripping over my lowered shorts and breaking a limb, or three, marred my joy at seeing the place where Jesus provided Peter with a bumper catch. It also occurred to me that this sanctified shorts-lowering might result in my marching onto the historic beach while sporting a very unholy builder's bottom. With difficulty I managed the maneuver without injury or (as far as I know) indecent exposure.

But how sad it is that visitors to this lovely place are greeted by such a stern prohibition – and this at the site where Jesus exuded such welcome, grace, kindness and care to his weary, worn-out fishing friends.

What first impressions do people get when they bump into me?

What first impressions do people get when they bump

into *me*? Is mine a life that quickly drops a hint of good news? And what about our churches (which are, of course, collectively what we are individually)? Do people feel genuine acceptance and welcome when they're around us, or do they sense that we're on the lookout for a better class of sinner?

I saw the hurt in the eyes of a young couple who were barred from the beach because of their summery shorts, and I wondered if we in the church have sent people packing in the name of cold, clinical holiness. Of course, hanging out with accomplished sinners will always get you into trouble, as Jesus most famously found out.

There was a final irony. When we left, I smiled at the holiness sentry who had warned me so sternly about my clothing selection. I had been so embarrassed, and upset that my knees might defile something, I hadn't noticed . . .

He was wearing shorts.

DAVID'S STORY

Perhaps, in most lifetimes, there are only six or seven days like them. They are the epic days, the crossroads that signal that everything is changing – and, most of all, the unalterable changes in us.

But these days dawn in ordinary hues just like any other. We do not awake on those mornings to the clanging of an alarm that warns us of what is about to come. Usually, no angel stands at our bedside to offer comfort or to inform us that this is a historic day. It is just time to get out of bed again. Only when we look back with the clarity of hindsight do we see how cataclysmically wonderful or tragic that particular day was.

As David stared into the bathroom mirror on such a morning in February 2003, he noticed that his right eye was very partially closed. Rubbing it, he wondered if he was suffering from some small infection – or maybe a **Sixteen-year-old boys are invincible** numbing clash of heads in last week's soccer game had caused his lazy eye and dull headache. Sixteen-year-old boys are invincible. They don't rush to fearful speculation with the nervous haste of those of us who have been around for a while and have learned that nobody is invincible. David was too busy with living at speed to get ill. A good-looking guy with a winning smile, he was an active member of his church, lead guitarist in a Christian band and an accomplished sportsman. But illness doesn't ask for a convenient appointment. Instead, it strikes with devastating disruption. There was a biopsy, and a shocking diagnosis. David was suffering from an aggressive cancer that was attacking the muscles around his right eye. He could be blinded, or worse.

David is the son of Stuart and Irene Bell, leaders of New Life Christian Fellowship in Lincoln, England. This large, thriving charismatic church is renowned for its vision, Bible teaching and balanced approach to faith. My wife Kay and I treasure the Bells as close, personal friends. Stuart also leads the Ground Level network, a coalition of churches scattered mainly around the Eastern seaboard of England. Every August, around nine thousand people gather for "Grapevine," a high-energy holiday weekend of worship and teaching.

The Bells are passionate believers. They had been through the fire of uncertainty and trial before, when Irene suffered a bungled surgery that led to eight more. They had faced that twilight period with fervent, prayerful hope. How would they cope with cancer attacking their youngest son?

I am nervous as I park outside the Leicester Royal Infirmary. This is the first day of David's many treatments; he has a long, arduous journey ahead of him. There will be nine courses of stomach-churning chemotherapy, painful bone marrow tests, a heart echo procedure, a bone scan, cat scans and, most embarrassing for a sixteen-year-old – a sperm count test. There will be too many days of wearying travel from Lincoln to Leicester. Radiotherapy will take its toll and David's schooling, in the year of his all-important final examinations, will be disrupted. He will not be able to complete most of these exams. This is where it all begins. The Bells are entering what must look like a long dark tunnel, and there is no certainty that they will all make it out to the light again.

As I hug the Bells, I am conscious of the unusual gift that I have brought for Stuart and Irene – a bottle of champagne, an incongruous present to be carrying into a cancer ward. I ask them to take the bottle home and place it somewhere prominent, to remind them to look for a better day, a celebration to come, when all this will be over. We laugh and cry. David is stretched out on the bed, delighting the nurses with his cheeky humor and waiting for it all to start. He grins broadly, but he is understandably nervous.

Stuart and I sit for awhile in the hospital café, stirring our lukewarm cups of tea. His cheeks are stained with tears, and his shoulders seem bowed by the pressure of this moment. A good father protects his child, but there is nothing that he can do to prevent the barrage of intrusive treatments that start today for David. But he can pray, and he does. I nod my heartfelt amen and sip my tea. There is not much that can be said that makes any sense. But Stuart is resolute: he is going to navigate this storm with a firm grip on God.

He is going to navigate this storm with a firm grip on God

An hour later, we are all laughing again. It's time for David's tests to begin, and so Stuart, David and I walk over to the sexual health clinic. I decide that it's time for me to lighten the proceedings, and so our walk to the clinic is peppered with predictably laddish humor. David has to answer some embarrassingly personal questions – in front of his dad – about the "procedure" to come, and finally he disappears into a room to do what has to be done. Stuart and I sit nervously in the waiting room. Finally he emerges, sample cup held high, and Stuart and I shatter the somber silence of the waiting room as we stand on our feet, clap our applause and cheer loudly. David laughs and the other patients wonder if we are mad.

Stuart and Irene had a problem. They believed that God was still in the business of physical healing, but they'd already limped through a traumatic few years during which Irene had been wheelchair-bound for a while. So how should they respond to this latest challenge? They wanted to remain open to God's miraculous intervention, and also to be balanced, realistic and responsible. The eyes of the church were upon them, and the steps they took would impact many. But, far more importantly, their son's life was in the balance and their primary responsibility was to minister to him. They urgently wanted to get this right. There were times of hesitation for Stuart. David would ask for assurance: "I will get well, won't I, Dad?" Stuart wanted to be absolutely truthful, yet totally hopeful. He affirmed that, yes, he believed that David would be well again.

To his disgust, David gained weight and his hair fell out

And Stuart put legs to his hopeful words as he called thirty close friends to daily, urgent prayer. Every night they would come together, alternately battling in urgent intercession and then gathering around David and taking loud authority over the cancer in his body. Stuart said succinctly, "We went to war." Sometimes people of faith have mistakenly dismissed the help of medical science, seeing prayer as the only legitimate answer. But this little band of prayerful warriors prayed for the doctors and specialists and thanked God for them. To his disgust, David gained weight and his hair fell out. Early scans were positive – the tumor seemed to be responding to treatment. Hopes were high, but fear was never far away.

It is the last night of Grapevine 2003. David, thirty-five pounds heavier now because of the treatments, and a black woolen hat disguising his baldness, has played a concert in one of the youth venues, and now his father's sermon is drawing to a close. Stuart has preached with power and insight on Paul's words to the Ephesians: "Stand firm on the evil day" (Eph. 6:13). Now Stuart calls Irene, and then David, to join him on stage. There is no hint of melodrama in this moment, just a simple, profound portrait of a family standing together in a time of huge pain. A song has particularly sustained David. It is "My glorious," by Delirious.

"God is bigger than the air I breathe, this world we'll leave.

God will save the day, and all will say, 'My glorious.'"

Thousands of voices cry out in prayer. God, please save David. Other family members and friends join the huddle on stage. Suddenly David reaches up and takes off his woolen hat, and his bald head gleams in the stage lights. God, please save David.

The crowds are long gone, I am now home in Colorado, and my mobile phone beeps. There is a message. It is David, who has always had a soft heart, but seems now to want to express himself with an openness not characteristic of a typical sixteen-year-old. His message is warm and funny, irreverent even, and then he signs off. "Actually Jeff, I really just telephoned to let you know that I love you. See you soon. Bye."

Months have rolled by, and the Bells have learned some unforgettable lessons. Fear is what we must fear, says Stuart. He has learned the power of hyperactive imagination, how just a flicker of concern spotted on the face of a cancer specialist can send a parent into a downhill spiral of depression and terror that can last for weeks.

They've also learned afresh the power of sustaining friendship, and they wonder how some families face such traumas without the support of prayerful friendship that church offers.

They are proud of their son, for their child has become not only a man, but a man of God

And they've discovered something that Stuart has dubbed "strange grace" – the special power that only shows up when we are at our wits' end. They are proud of their son, for their child has become not only a man, but a man of God.

They have watched their son get on with life as best as he could, playing in the worship team, attending practices, playing soccer when energy levels allowed it – business as usual. Cancer is always an unwelcome visitor, a fearsome stalker - but life has to go on even as you fight it. The mortgage still needs paying, the church still calls for leadership, and life doesn't press a pause button while great battles are fought. The fight is an additional pressure.

The results are good – very good indeed. David will need to endure frequent check-ups for a long time to come, but all trace of the cancer is gone. There is a celebratory party, and there are balloons and streamers and champagne bottles everywhere. I am invited to speak, and I talk about bar mitzvah, the coming of age of a young man. Prayer warriors are thanked, and then the Bells invite a smiling group of doctors and nurses to step onto the platform. They are wildly applauded for being the heroes that they really are.

Later that night in the Bell's home, a bottle of champagne is lifted off the mantle where it has stood for fifteen months, and we pop the cork and share a prayer of thanksgiving. And this was no naive toast. We raised our glasses with the full knowledge that others are called to celebrate when their prayers are not answered as they wanted. Today, some will lift up their eyes to the God who did not spare their loved ones from death, but in death.

Fear lingers longer than cancer, so there are times when David stares into the mirror for a very long time in the mornings, wondering if another epic day has dawned. But all really is well.

There have been some unexpected bonuses from the unwelcome and unwanted journey. A children's charity arranged for David to meet Elton John, and then Eric Clapton. Photographs of him with the two rock legends proudly adorn the family home. And there have been some unexpected battles, too – with an irrational guilt, because he has survived when many others have succumbed to the evil that is cancer.

But David, you are the youngest hero in my life. You met the challenges head-on, were honest about your fears, held onto God with a tenacious grip, and showed me – and many others – that faith works best when you find yourself in the furnace. You have learned, at such a young age, how to live life out loud. Your hair has grown back, the extra pounds are shed and you have a beautiful girlfriend in Sarah. The cancer has been tamed: but you are left with a fighter's heart.

God certainly is "our glorious one, who lifts up our heads"

God certainly is "our glorious one, who lifts up our heads." I'll never forget the night that we sang that together. And David – you taught me that those are far more than great, biblical lyrics to a wonderful worship song.

It's the truth.